DATING DISASTERS

AND HOW TO AVOID THEM

Also by Dr. Joy Browne

~~~~~

Dating for Dummies

The Field Experience (contributor)

Getting Unstuck (available from Hay House)

It's a Jungle Out There, Jane

**The Nine Fantasies That Will Ruin Your Life
(and the Eight Realities that Will Save You)**

Nobody's Perfect: How to Stop Blaming and Start Living

The Used Car Game

Why They Don't Call When They Say They Will

~~~~~

Please visit Hay House USA: **www.hayhouse.com**
Hay House Australia: **www.hayhouse.com.au**
Hay House UK: **www.hayhouse.co.uk**
Hay House South Africa: **orders@psdprom.co.za**

DATING DISASTERS

AND HOW TO AVOID THEM

Dr. Joy Browne

HAY HOUSE, INC.
Carlsbad, California
London • Sydney • Johannesburg
Vancouver • Hong Kong

Published and distributed in the United States by: Hay House, Inc., P.O. Box 5100, Carlsbad, CA 92018-5100 • *Phone:* (760) 431-7695 or (800) 654-5126 • *Fax:* (760) 431-6948 or (800) 650-5115 • www.hayhouse.com • **Published and distributed in Australia by:** Hay House Australia Pty. Ltd., 18/36 Ralph St., Alexandria NSW 2015 • *Phone:* 612-9669-4299 • *Fax:* 612-9669-4144 • www.hayhouse.com.au • **Published and distributed in the United Kingdom by:** Hay House UK, Ltd. • Unit 62, Canalot Studios • 222 Kensal Rd., London W10 5BN • *Phone:* 44-20-8962-1230 • *Fax:* 44-20-8962-1239 • www.hayhouse.co.uk • **Published and distributed in the Republic of South Africa by:** Hay House SA (Pty), Ltd., P.O. Box 990, Witkoppen 2068 • *Phone/Fax:* 27-11-706-6612 • orders@psdprom.co.za • **Distributed in Canada by:** Raincoast • 9050 Shaughnessy St., Vancouver, B.C. V6P 6E5 • *Phone:* (604) 323-7100 • *Fax:* (604) 323-2600

Design: Jenny Richards

Library of Congress Cataloging-in-Publication Data

Browne, Joy.
Dating disasters and how to avoid them / by Joy Browne.
p. cm.
ISBN 1-4019-0524-2 (hardcover) — ISBN 1-4019-0525-0 (tradepaper) 1. Dating (Social customs)
2. Men– Psychology. 3. Man-woman relationships. I. Title.
HQ801.B8678 2005
646.7'7—dc22

2004005756

Hardcover ISBN 13: 978-1-4019-0524-8
Hardcover ISBN 10: 1-4019-0524-2
Tradepaper ISBN 10: 1-4019-0525-0
Tradepaper ISBN 13: 978-1-4019-0525-5

08   07   06   05   5   4   3   2
1st printing, January 2005
2nd printing, April 2005

Printed in the United States of America

~~~

To:

*Those who believe that
the phrase "dating disasters"
is redundant.*

*Those who hope like crazy
that it's not.*

This one's for you.

~~~

Contents

Introduction ix

PART I: TYPES OF GUYS

Chapter 1: *The Too-Good-to-Be-Trues* 3
The Married Guy • The Separated-but-Still-Married Guy
• The Recently Divorced Guy • The Stuck Guy

Chapter 2: *The Dance-Away Lover* 21
The Game Player • The Addict • The Manic-Depressive

Chapter 3: *A Decalogue of Dunces* 31
The Mama's Boy • The Passive-Aggressive • The Whiner
• The Control Freak • The Misogynist • The Competitor
• The Narcissist • The Trust-Fund Kid • The Gold Digger
• The Self-Loather

Chapter 4: *The Good Guy* 59

PART II: DOOM-A-DATE

Chapter 5: *First Impressions* 65
Chapter 6: *The First Date: Part I* 71
How? • Where? • When?
• What (Am I Going to Wear)? • Who?

Chapter 7: *The First Date: Part II* 81
Time • Attitude • Conversation • Chemistry
• Personal Hygiene • Money

Chapter 8: *The Next Toxic Step: Nine Power Tools* 105
Bullying • Anger • Arguments • Tantrums • Sarcasm •
Arrogance • Criticism • Jealousy • Pretense

PART III: DISASTROUS DATING COMMANDMENTS

Chapter 9: Get Engaged on Groundhog Day 133
Chapter 10: Believe in Soul Mates and Love at First Sight 137
Chapter 11: Invest Heavily in the Beginning .141
Chapter 12: Meet a Man on a Plane
(Especially One That's Going Through Turbulence) 145
Chapter 13: Assume That Sex Means Anything 149
Chapter 14: Count Condoms 153
Chapter 15: Date Outside Your Area Code 155
Chapter 16: Give a Man a Cow (Overwhelm Him) 161
Chapter 17: Lie about the Small Things 167
Chapter 18: Assume That You Can Change Him 171

In Closing 173
Acknowledgments 181
About the Author 183

INTRODUCTION

People will tell us everything we need to know about them in the first 15 minutes—most of us just don't pay any attention to the information we get. The most extreme case of this disastrous tendency (the ignoring, not the communicating) is when we're dating. In addition to the stress and excitement of meeting and reacting to a stranger with potential romantic interest, we're busy presenting who we want to come off as: likable, lovable, cute, sexy, and sane. We see less of who the other people are because we're so nervous about who *we* are.

Dating would be ever so much easier if everybody had their own agenda tattooed on their chest (or at least emblazoned on a T-shirt). Thus, we'd easily be able to watch out for "Playboy looking for a good time," "Career woman who needs an escort but doesn't want children," "Needy doormat seeks father figure," or "Titan of the universe desires arm candy." Unfortunately, what we're shown is a bit more subtle. Nevertheless, I'm going to teach you how to read people as if everybody was walking around with who they are and what they want printed out for all to see. As far as I'm concerned, you can still ignore the information if you want to, but at least you'll know how to access it if you choose to.

"Dating Disasters" is actually a double entendre: First of all, you can certainly date a disaster, but even if the guy isn't a mess, you can make any dating situation a disaster all by yourself. Usually when I write a book about relationships, I spend lots of time explaining how to avoid potentially heart-breaking situations, but in this book, I'll tell you how to *find* and *guarantee* them. So, if you want to make sure that you'll always be alone on Christmas or have some dude borrow and never repay serious money from you, I've got the perfect guy for you.

Are you looking for a shiftless layabout so that you're always the one paying the bills, or a spineless Mama's boy? Together, we'll find you one to cherish. In other words, I'm going to teach you exactly how you can wreck your love life, if you so desire. I'll help you identify men who will depress you, abandon you, and demean you, as well as show you where and how to spot them. In case you don't think you can find guys to break your heart on your own, not to worry—Dr. Joy is here to help you find someone who will stomp on it, BBQ it, and eat it for breakfast.

So, Part I of this handy little guide outlines how to spot a disaster in the wild. To begin, I've adopted the gimmick that we can actually decode the personal ad of a certain type of guy. How a man describes himself is consistent with how he'll present himself to you, so you'll learn how to spot the ones who will make you miserable—that way, you can scope out and identify the bait they toss out, and observe them in their natural habitats. Next, I'll outline the advantages and disadvantages of each guy and the best way to deal with him, and lead you through the most likely scenario of the dude's routines and modus operandi. Finally, you'll learn both what to do and what not to do if, once you've got him, you're determined to lose (or keep) him.

What if you're not into terminal masochism—is there anyone out there for you? The answer, of course, is yes. I'll show you exactly how to identify a good guy—one who's worked out his issues with his parents, has been out of any serious relationship for at least a year, and has the same philosophy on children that you have (either he wants them if you do or he doesn't if you don't)—so that you and he can then have a "Velcro relationship," with as many points in common as possible.

However, if you'd prefer to destroy even the best of relationships, Parts II and III will outline procedures you should follow to ensure a dating disaster. You'll also get to take me with you on that first date: I'll be your eyes, sharpening your gaze and honing your perceptions.

Since I spend so much time telling you about situations that should be avoided like the plague, I've also provided ample advice for "Avoiding Disasters." Here, you can view me as your little love cherub, floating down to paste lace around your left ventricle, whispering in your shell-pink ear how to avoid a bad situation or a certain dilemma. For example, if your friends point out that your perpetual tardiness drives them wild, you might flirt with the notion of promptness on a date; if you're fidgety about waiting, you could take a book and relax—seemingly straightforward advice, yes? But for those of you who are heavily into the "duh" factor, that's what divine intervention is all about: to tell you exactly what to do to make things *better* rather than *worse* . . . or even worse rather than better should you so desire.

Lookin' for Love . . . in Cyberspace

In this book, I'd like you to pretend that your first introduction to your date is online. I came up with this idea for a number of reasons. First, an awful lot of people these days are actually meeting and dating online (estimates are 45 million Americans, which translates into 50 percent of all couples), although not all admit to it publicly.

So if we assume that online descriptions are the best way to understand who we are and what we want, then the path to dating disasters becomes clear. I stated in the very first sentence of this Introduction that people will tell us everything we need to know about them in the first 15 minutes, but we pay no attention. To prove my point, I'll show you how most will tell us everything we need to know about them in the first 15 *words,* and we're still oblivious. Don't take my word for it—on the next page are honest-to-goodness, real-life, online ads, which have been reprinted verbatim (poor grammar, creative spelling, and cringe-worthy syntax has been left as discovered . . .).

You think these guys are kidding, looking to surprise or shock. But these ideas had to come from somewhere in their demented little minds. *Beware.* (Point proved about using online sites as a useful dating model that allows for instant access to the heart and soul of the matter, right?)

LOOKIN' FOR A HOT MAMA

I'm a generally easy-goin guy. I say generally, cause sometimes I let my temper get out of hand. I like to break things, specially when I've been a drinkin' a little much. Don't let that scare you, though . . . there's still a lot of lovin' to go around. Don't expect me to look as good as my photo; I had to go and get all cleaned up for this. I'm not particular. I've been involved with many women over the years. Some I can't even remember what they looked like. Oh well, I say. The way I see it, the more particular I am, the longer it takes to hook up.

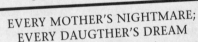

EVERY MOTHER'S NIGHTMARE; EVERY DAUGTHER'S DREAM

Total Mr. Wrong . . . charming, funny, generous, totally unavailable. Three vices—expensive cigars, beautiful cars, and fast women. (Or something like that.) Seeking an educated, literate, intelligent woman who enjoys (and is accomplished at) flirting, witty conversation and would love a dalliance with a total Mr. Wrong. Want kids: No way!

LOOKING TO HAVE SOME FUN

Please excuse the photo, it is just the most recent one I had. The lady I'm with is just a "Chatty Kathy" and the wife of a friend. We were at a party, somebody said let's take a picture and there you are.

Essentially, *Dating Disasters* is written for grown-ups (if you're under the age of 21, don't read on—it will depress the daylights out of you and convince you to take those final vows of celibacy at the convent); I also assume that at some point, somebody did you wrong. But the question is: Can you move beyond that? Can you take that shriveled, bruised little heart of yours into battle as your shield and symbol? If you want to ensure disaster, don't let me stand in your way, but if you'd rather have a fighting chance, it may make sense to understand these types, the patterns, and yourself.

One more major caveat before we proceed. The personal ads in this first section are all real . . . and all about men. Before you assume that I'm seriously into male bashing or one of those man haters you read about, let me assure you that women also write dumb personal ads, and have some annoying little tics, to say the least, that can doom dating. However, it became unwieldy to talk about both men and women in the same book. Therefore, the choice to include only male profiles here was made for several reasons: (1) The ratio of male to female ads on the Internet is wildly disproportionate; (2) there's a lot already written on how women types mess things up—or you can watch ten minutes of any television sitcom; and (3) since women are so much more prone to navel-gazing and self-analysis, I thought I'd shower the guys with attention.

So women, listen up; and men, make sure that you're not reading about yourself here. Also, for any of you contemplating writing a personal ad, learn what not to do . . . unless you're seriously into catastrophes.

The rest of this book focuses on ways that *both* men and women can louse things up. Here we go!

PART I

Types
of Guys

CHAPTER 1
The Too-Good-to-Be-Trues

Many women nowadays assume that all men are commitment-phobes, avoiding intimacy like an emotional root canal—in other words, anyone with a Y chromosome and testosterone will play hard to get, lie about any- and everything, put work first, won't ever call, be fixated on Mom and/or his ex, and be out playing the field. Men are all believed to be serial daters on the lookout for bimbos, not real women; they want a one-nighter, not one true love; and they're more interested in "afternoon delight" than an eternal partnership.

Enter the fellow who's too good to be true: He seems genuinely interested without being pathetically overeager. He makes eye contact without making sexual advances or crude comments. He's respectful, has good manners, and offers to take you to nice places rather than his apartment on the first date. He calls or e-mails you regularly. He seems to be neither a starving artist nor a megalomaniac. He doesn't introduce you to his friends, yet he does seem to actually have some. He wants to talk about things you're interested in, he listens, and he asks you how your day was. He seems like a gentleman who's completely thrilled by your independence, yet he's also tolerant of your occasional neediness. He asks no questions about your sexual history, is accepting of your child/best friend/mother, and is neither possessive nor jealous of you.

This guy is either the find of a lifetime, or he's too good to be true because he's got something else going on for him: a wife. He's been domesticated, so he's learned what women want, how to present himself, and how to couch his demands in requests. You may say to yourself, "Well, maybe he just has a great mom." Yeah, yeah, yeah . . . *everybody's* got a great mom (and we'll talk about moms in great detail later on), but it's much more likely that he has the mom of the universe, a.k.a. his wife. This means that he can afford to be the most charming man who seems completely interested in you, without having any concern about your entrapping him or making assumptions about his availability. He can seem to put it all on the line because really, nothing for him is. He's already spoken for.

You're going to call your mom or your friends and say, "I just met this great guy who's genuinely interested in me," but you very likely haven't asked the obvious question, which is, "Are you single? Available? Living with somebody? Separated? Recently divorced? In love with somebody? Getting over a breakup?" By not asking any of those questions, you make it very easy to swallow the bait of this man's availability, which is only a fantasy. *He isn't available.*

Certainly, the way to make yourself miserable is to fall madly in love with this guy, who will be very appealing to you because he knows exactly what bait to use. After all, it worked once, and he's had a long time to perfect his technique. . . .

But this book isn't about abstractions; it's about real guys with real pitches. (Okay, I did edit them down occasionally, since lots of them were really long and I had to change a detail or two if I felt I was going to otherwise get sued, but for the most part, what you see is what I found, unvarnished and delicious. If you recognize yourself or someone you know or have dated, odds are you're right!) So without further ado, let's meet, up close and personal, some real-life too-good-to-be-trues.

The Married Guy

MY WIFE DOESN'T UNDERSTAND ME
I know you've heard it all before, but my wife really doesn't understand me. We've been in a loveless, sexless marriage for years, but financial situations and my position in the community make divorce impossible. I can be the kind, loving, generous, sexy lover you've always wanted. Looking for an independent, self-reliant woman who knows that life is short and pleasure is to be grabbed and indulged.

Why would any woman in her right mind respond to this guy? Whoops, I forgot—we're talking about dating disasters here! And seeing a married man should be at the top of that hit parade.

The Married Guy will give you all sorts of explanations as to why you shouldn't consider the fact that he's hitched to be a disadvantage, and if you really want to be miserable, follow his lead. He'll convince you that his wife doesn't understand him. (Believe it or not, some guy actually tried that line on me. I burst into giggles and said, "Lucky you!") He'll tell you that he thought you were a modern woman who wasn't concerned about silly conventions like marriage. He'll explain that he and the little woman are together in name only, haven't had sex in years, or have an "arrangement" (that is, they live in the same house but lead separate lives). They're waiting for the kids to grow up, graduate, get married, or die. His wife has major emotional problems and hasn't been a real spouse to him in years. He's afraid she can't function or afford to live on her own. Neither of them have the nerve to tell their parents, or they're prominent members of the community and would lose their social standing. He'll come up with every creative notion there is as to why it's okay for him to be married and, essentially, commit adultery with you.

Married men are catnip—especially to needy women—because they seem to provide everything. You think, *Here's a guy who tells me I'm the most wonderful person he's ever met and that I make him feel special, which makes me feel good about myself,* but the reason he can do all this is because he's married!

First of all, we know that he's capable of commitment—he's married. Second, we know that he doesn't have to put anything on the line because he's married. So if you're unfortunate enough to get involved with this guy and he's still living with his wife, then you're a moron. If he'll cheat on his wife, he'll cheat on you; therefore, you can't view him as a long-term commitment at all. If you're really determined to date a married man, then you needn't read any further because you've already perfected a recipe for disaster. Just go buy yourself a giant supply of waterproof mascara and settle in. You're going to be spending a lot of time sitting by the phone, waiting for him to call with tears running down your cheeks, and being dissed by your friends, who've heard the story for the 80th time.

The married man is fairly straightforward: He has no intention of leaving his wife and may even tell you as much. But the next man we're going to meet is in a slightly different, but even scarier, category.

The Separated-but-Still-Married Guy

SEPARATED, LOOKING FOR COMPANY

I am recently separated. We got along fine until we got married, then she changed. I'm looking for someone that will lay all their cards on the table from the start. Don't tell me you like something just because I do, and you want to please me. If you don't like it, tell me. . . . About me, I am an easy-going person. I hate bringing my job home. I would like to meet someone that likes to go out and have fun. And you have to be decisive—if I ask your opinion about something it's because I want to hear it, a joint decision is better than always doing what one person wants.

This guy's got a chip on his shoulder the size of Des Moines—and guess who will be asked to go around it, over it, or try like crazy to reduce it to gravel? You, my little cupcake.

Away from the personals, this type may manifest himself as the soon-to-be-divorced, handsome, professional, passionate male with full custody of a six-year-old boy. He'll tell you that he and his son are a package deal: He's looking for friends who want to have fun with both of them, so his time is limited. "When we get the chance to do something, we make the best of our time together," he'll say. "If you like to have fun and enjoy being with kids, come and join us. I love to cook, and I try to keep a clean house (as much as I can with a six-year-old), and I'm very handy. Do you need a Mr. Fixit? I try my best with broken hearts."

Touching, right? Wrong. He's still married, and is interviewing for an unpaid nanny, cook, housekeeper, and "fun" person. As for your needs—sorry, there's no time.

That nice-looking man you keep seeing at the dog park will tell you that he's just looking for a companion, since he and his wife have been separated for six months. He'll get a bit misty-eyed when he mentions how much he misses his 14-year-old daughter, who's staying with his wife in an apartment in another town, and all he wants is someone who could help understand what he may have done wrong. In other words, he's still married. *Beware.*

Or you may find a sweet, hardworking guy who likes bowling, fishing, baseball, and the great outdoors, but he's only available on Sundays. Well, this is a man who may have already moved out of the family household, but you're going to have to deal with all sorts of issues. You're going to be his emotional Red Cross, making concessions that you wouldn't normally make under healthier circumstances. He won't be able to afford dinner, vacations, or birthday presents because he's "going through a divorce" that he either hasn't filed or finalized yet. He may or may not be legally separated (many states don't have such a thing), but regardless, he ain't single.

The biggest problem with this guy, lest you miss my point: He's still married. He may not be living with his wife, and he may not even like the woman, but he's still lawfully tied to someone else. In other words, this dude has financial, relationship, parental, and legal issues to deal with (not to mention who gets the dog). So even a man who may no longer be living with his wife needs to be considered still married until the divorce is *final*—not pending or in process.

You may consider the Separated-but-Still-Married Guy one step up from the man who says he's not going to leave his wife, but at least the Married Guy is being honest with you. In some ways, the Still-Married Guy is the scariest of married men because even if he's in process (and let's give him the benefit of the doubt at this moment and say that he does intend to get divorced), he'll still be going through an unsettled, adolescent time.

I'm sure you remember how emotional and flaky you were during your own adolescence, when you could no longer accept the constraints around you. You knew that where you were was only going to be temporary, but you didn't really understand how it was going to be when you were completely out from under the situation. That's why teenagers are such unpredictable, unlikable people.

Now do you really want to be involved with somebody who's going through a marital adolescence? This guy sees where he was and clearly doesn't want to be there, and he doesn't want to be with his wife anymore—but understand that you're both going to be haunted by whoever she was. That is, if she was always late, then the first time you're even five minutes tardy, he's going to be all over you like white on rice. If she was somebody who had "headaches," then the first time you don't want to have sex with him, he'll view you as being just as cold as she was. It's a very treacherous time for you, and you may find that this guy has all the control because you're always auditioning for him.

He's also going to be dealing with a ton of baggage—for example, he's going to have to see his kids all the time because they're traumatized. If his "not-ex" wife calls, he's going to say he owes her. It's very likely that he's going to be with her on her birthday, their anniversary, and Christmas, whether it be for the kids, for him, for the in-laws, or for his own guilt. You're going to be haunted by her ghost, and she isn't dead . . . for either of you.

Furthermore, people *have* been known to reconcile. But even if they don't get back together, he won't view himself as divorced until the paperwork comes through, so his meter will start running then—even though yours has been running for a very long time. In other words, by the time he really is divorced, he's going to want to be single. Just as you're thinking, *Wow, this guy is finally available. I'm ready, and he's ready,* he's going to want to be on his own for a while. You've made him realize that there are great women out there who will not only tolerate him, but will love and have sex with him, too. So why settle into a marriage or serious relationship with all its potential pitfalls again so soon?

Now, understand that his personal ad is going to say: "Long walks on the beach. I want a friend. I want a true partner," which sounds too good to be true. But if he's honest, he'll also say, "I'm not ready for monogamy," because even if he's in the much-to-be-hoped-for-but-nearly-as-ambiguous status of "in the process of divorce," it's still a synonym for "married." This dude isn't available—and not only is he not available now, he's not going to be available anytime in the near future . . . which brings us to our next candidate.

The Recently Divorced Guy

RECENTLY SINGLE (DIVORCED) AND LOOKING TO HAVE SOME WELL-DESERVED FUN

I was faithfully married for many years only to find out it was one sided and she was only interested in money. I am now looking for someone who shares MY interests and is willing to just spend time with me and enjoy the simpler things in life. My only vice (so I'm told) is I like beer. I have no formal education, but have a Ph.D. in the school of life. I'm looking for someone to spend quality time with. Walking, talking, sipping a drink, shooting a game of pool, fishing, shooting guns, listening to music, traveling, snow-mobiling, motor-cycling, solving the problems of the universe, and having great sex.

Okay, cookie, you don't even need to read between the lines here—Mr. My Way or the Highway has laid it all out plain and simple, and woe be to you if your interests don't mesh with his. But what I'm about to say doesn't only apply to the guy placing the ad above—it's for anybody who hasn't been well and truly out of a marriage, which is minimally a year after the divorce is final.

If you've ever dissolved a marriage, then you know how chaotic the year following a divorce is; if you haven't, well, trust me, it is—and you don't want to be part of somebody else's chaos. As a construction worker once said to me, "When you see a project under construction, cross the street because it's dangerous. Things can fly off and hit you in the head, which is why we wear hard hats." Well, you can't wear a hard hat around your heart, so just stay away from guys whose divorce is less than a year old.

A shortcut to disaster is to simply break the One-Year Rule (which is the thing that I'm the most loathed for in the entire world). Take it from me both personally and professionally: The quickest way to Heartbreak City is to date someone before the first anniversary of their divorce. I can hear you whining, "But they were separated for months first. What's the big deal?" I don't care if they've been separated since dirt was invented—"separated" still equals "married." Until the divorce goes through, there's no tearing asunder of the tie, those vows they made in front of all of their friends, relatives, and God; with special food, with special dress, in a special place, and at great expense; with the state actually licensing the whole deal. Marriage is a big-time, full-tilt-boogie serious commitment; consequently, divorce can be a sometimes liberating but often painful, and certainly life-changing, experience, so people need to take time to "decathect" or disconnect. Allow me to explain this concept further.

When you're in a relationship with another human being, you send out little connecting ties. When you smile at somebody, you send out little baby tendrils; when you shake hands with somebody, you send out more connections; and when you have a fourth date with someone, you've sent out a stronger kind of entanglement. Marriage is a kind of encapsulation of two people together, in which they're separate from others and really entangled with each other. Most ceremonies talk about making the two one; about sharing a name, a home, and a commitment; about abandoning all others and clinging to that one other person. And when, for whatever reason, that relationship goes south, there's a major feeling of loss.

Humans aren't like vacuum cleaners: We can't just press a button and—*thwup!*—all our little tendrils quickly return to the fold, leaving us whole and ready to rumble again. When an unhappy, recently dumped friend says, "I feel like a part of me is missing," she's describing a very accurate physical metaphor for a psychological reality. In any relationship, no matter how lousy, we do connect with another person, and when that relationship falls apart, we don't instantly spring back to ourselves right away. We need time to heal, to feel less wounded, to strengthen, and to become ourselves again.

After the relationship has been formally put asunder (generally by death, loss, or divorce), it takes us a while to find our sea legs again and discover who we are following the experience—and until we do so, we're going to be very needy. Need is a fabulously efficient blueprint for both initial involvement and long-term disaster. If you're needy, and I provide, then I've taken care of your needs immediately. But for the relationship to continue once you're not needy anymore, one of two things is going to happen: (1) Your need for me goes away, so you go away; or (2) I'm going to feel that I have to remind you of what I provided before—that is, make you feel guilty and beholden or force you to cling to me once again by making you feel inadequate, belittling you, and reminding you that you were more likable as the person you were before.

Supply and need are terrific tools for disaster: While initially they dovetail quite neatly and make it seem like you and your intended were meant for each other for the short term, they can't work for any length of time. So, if you want to ensure misery, be certain that you launch yourself into any kind of relationship by requesting that someone else provide for you. Asking someone to be your emotional, financial, social, sexual, and intellectual support will allow you to put yourself in a position of great vulnerability . . . and we all know how well animals respond to a show of weakness. You're either going to find a predator, a bully, or someone who must feel superior or needed or both. Just in case you're worried that disaster could be avoided, that neediness could evolve into a more balanced relationship, rest assured that the odds and the work necessary to crawl out of that hole make it very unlikely.

Now, anyone who takes a year off and chooses to focus on themselves rather than dating will have gone through a Christmas, a Fourth of July, and a birthday keeping their own company. They'll have hung out with friends, been a volunteer, and spent time with family—then, after that year is over, they'll be in a better position to evaluate their *wants* rather than their *needs* . . . which means that they'll be ready to commit to a solid, real relationship. Unfortunately, we can't say the same for our next gentleman.

The Stuck Guy

SINGLE, NOT DIVORCED . . . READY TO GO!

I'm tall, user friendly, was married for 24 years . . . but 13 years ago the mother of our 4 children wanted to "find herself" (still lookin'). I chose to throw myself into my work & now consider myself single not divorced . . . it's not a condition but something that took place w/o my consent. I know what a good relationship (bond) w/the opposite sex is . . . ready to get on w/my life. Looking for someone with little or no emotional baggage and (probably?) has been previously married. Such as a widow or a "dumpee" that has experienced, if but for only a few years, a good marriage and thus knows what a true "relationship" is like. With reference to "kids" it evolves out of the fact that I can communicate w/children easier than adults. Plus they're open & honest about their feelings. If they think your ugly they'll tell you, etc. She is not looking for a one night stand or "Mr. Right Now." NO she doesn't have to walk on water . . . I've tried & can't do it yet, but I am trying to earn my wings.

This dude has been divorced for more than half the time he was married—yet after more than a decade, he's still bearing a major-league grudge, as well as a brightly burning torch.

Of course, not every guy is quite so blatant about his emotional unavailability. He may couch his need for you in metaphors or sports analogies, but make no mistake: You'll never come first—or even second—in his life. He wants you to be self-reliant enough to take care of yourself and him . . . oh, and by the way, he'd like you to be a real mother figure for his son.

That's right: He may be passionate with you, but his real love is his kid(s). He'll tell you that he's happiest when making his seven-year-old son happy, then he'll bashfully tell you that he doesn't think men are genetically coded to nurture children: "I think that women are more consistent," he'll say. "You have an internal natural discipline when it comes to meals, baths, bedtime . . . everything. My son is so happy and well adjusted, and he's a good student. Emotionally, I excel with him, but I'm going by memories of my wife when it comes to the daily caring for him. It's a struggle not to raise another bachelor. So, how about helping us out here?"

The Stuck Guy is charming, but deadly. You can't win 'cause you're competing with wife memories. And since this is his focus and his goal, you'll be evaluated as a mom first and everything else second—and his kid will have veto power. This man will make no bones about the fact that his most important self-definition is as a great father, because that's first and foremost the most treasured aspect of his life. As far as he's concerned, his priority is his children.

Under the guise of being a good daddy, he may also have kept in *really* close touch with Mom. That means that the cute new guy in your apartment building may have moved in just to be with his children (and one very happy ex-wife). He'll warn you that you must understand that his children are a big part of his life and not to let that be a conflict. "My ex-wife and I are friends and we get along well. I loved having someone to come home to, and I'm ready to settle down again with the right woman." Let's see . . . spending time with the ex-wife on the weekends, with the kids as a package deal— yikes!

And while this guy is blatant in his needs, men who are in transition are always needy, which can be expressed in surprisingly seductive ways. He seems too good to be true because he's capable of commitment—after all, he's been married before. He knows how to live with a woman. He knows how to behave around women: He'll hold an umbrella up for you in the rain; and help you with your coat, car door, and PMS. He's domesticated, so he'll be nice to your mom, remember your anniversary, and buy you tampons.

However, he can only go so far because he's still crying about his wife; he's still angry, and he's still fighting. He's fighting over the house, he's fighting over the money, he's fighting over the kids, and he's fighting over the dogs. Sooner or later, any conversation will go back to the divorce and the fact that he hasn't healed from it yet.

A subtle way for a man to hang on to his old life is to delude himself that he and his kids (of any age) are best friends. While I'm all in favor of adults working out a relationship with their children, any man who thinks that his kids are his best friends doesn't have adult pals of his own. In addition, part of what he's talking about is a control issue. A child's willingness to indulge a parental fantasy of best chums is often based on the Golden Rule: "He who has the gold, rules." In other words, I'd be willing to bet that he's paying the bills for his kids *and* his ex-wife, and he's stuck.

This guy is stuck in an area where he can have all the control and all the outward manifestations of having a rich emotional life without any of the intimacy. This is a man who's not going to make room for anybody new in his life because anytime he's feeling any kind of closeness, which is challenging to him (and intimacy is challenging to us all), he's going to immediately wrap himself in his kids or in his ex to feel safe. He's already lost everything he's going to lose there, so while it might feel a bit deficient to him, it also feels utterly familiar and safe.

For instance, my friend dated a guy who, during their first weekend away together, ended up tearfully expressing regrets over missing his 30-year-old son's birthday. The man lived across the country from his son and hadn't been with him on his birthday for five years—yet every square inch of his home was covered with artifacts and reminders of his boy. Holidays were spent with his ex, whom he bad-mouthed (at least to my friend), yet this same ex also lived in his house, answering his phone and presumably his mail when he traveled. There was no room in his life for anything new.

Sure, the Stuck Guy is perfect if you love to hear stories about his family, and while a guy who's cheery about his ex-wife is threatening on some level, a guy who's furious is just as irritating. Beware: Stuck is stuck, even if it's fury covered with a sticky-sweet frosting of "Look at me, I'm happy!" Guess who's going to be the lightning rod, recipient, and, in his mind, the cause of all that barely concealed rage? You, honey bear, nobody but you!

Just remember: If he seems too good to be true, *he is.*

CHAPTER 2

The Dance-Away Lover

Welcome to the suitor who will move in and out of your life—as he feels you getting close to him, he'll be gone before you know what hit you. Intimacy for this guy is all fake: He'll be charming, affectionate, sensual, and accommodating sexually, which is part of the game. He wants to move you in close enough to feel that somehow he's acceptable and lovable. You'll be the sun that warms his cold, cold heart, but getting too close threatens his existence. Ladies, meet the Dance-Away Lover.

PLAYFUL, FLIRTATIOUS, SECRETIVE

Where to begin? My female friends would enumerate my defining characteristics as playful, flirtatious, secretive (they all think I lead a double life—I keep telling them to stop with the prying personal questions and I will stop with my decidedly vague answers), always on the go and will never settle down (of course they have all been smitten with me at one time or another and are all a little bitter)! You have to keep me laughing to keep my interest peaked (it does require an intelligent sense of humor)! I do want to settle down, I just don't know when. I have a talent for making spontaneous weekend trips (3–4 days) happen . . . far off islands, remote mountain getaways, big city excursions—I don't discriminate! I am most attracted to women who are independent, ambitious, and who can add something to the mix socially and intellectually.

Remember, gentle reader, this is a real-life person's description of himself. At a party, this guy is often the center of attention. He seems quirky and funny and is always into some new project—whether it's writing, a new sport, or even you. He'll admit that he's somewhat erratic and even a teensy bit grandiose, but he's clear about needing space. He wants you to be a stable personality, but one who yearns for adventure and excitement at the same time—which is some sort of balance that he thinks he lacks. Be forewarned.

Then there's the flirt who couches his unreliability in seeming sophistication. He'll buy you the latest hip concoction, know the "in" places, and talk about "a mutuality of spirit that's a match for our depth of experience, individuality, and uniqueness. What counts for us is the comfort of friendship. You'll love my ability to perceive who you are and to be responsive, caring, and supportive of your feelings, thoughts, and behaviors. You're independent, not looking to be saved, pacified, or condescended to. In summary, you live from the presence that you are: animated, open, and loving. Oh, and by the way—I'm *not* looking for a monogamous relationship."

Oh, goody—he's responsive, caring, and supportive . . . unless you trouble your pretty little head with thoughts of venereal disease, loyalty, trust, and somebody to spend New Year's Eve with.

The Dance-Away Lover isn't obvious at the beginning because, like the Separated-but-Still-Married Guy, he seems too good to be true at first glance. He'll be charming. He'll listen to you. He'll take you where you want to go— even to your mother's birthday party. The problem with this guy is that he's addicted to the game, which is to get you in close . . . but only so close.

He can't tolerate real intimacy because he doesn't like himself—and he fears that you won't like the "real" guy any better than he does. And the closer you get, the greater the risk of exposure. He'll take you away for a long weekend, then break up with you on Monday. After great sex, he'll have to go home. You'll feel completely vulnerable because he's made it very clear that he wants you to be close—but he can only tolerate it to a very limited extent, which he'll make painfully clear when you least expect it.

He's great at talking and knows all the right words. He's a "perfect guy" pro, so when he disappears, you'll react as if *you* did something wrong— you'll call him up to apologize and make everything all right. But he'll then reinforce your sense of wrongness by telling you that you're crowding him and are asking too much of him, and he's not really ready for this level of commitment. You'll both agree that it's your fault. However, once you back out, he'll come running after you because for him, it's all a matter of seduction, the push-pull, getting you close enough that he feels your warmth again and feels valuable . . . yet as soon as he does, he'll back off once more.

Now understand that he's really not trying to make you feel foolish. He isn't tuned in to your vulnerability per se, but to his own sense of inadequacy. If you tell him that his behavior is hurting you, he won't be touched at all— and if you tell him that he's breaking your heart, he'll say that his hurts more. He's urgently aware of his own inadequacies, and yours aren't even a distant second. This guy is incapable of intimacy because he's incapable of finding a safe place in his own psyche to stand.

Now this category of disastrous date can be further broken down into the Game Player, the Addict, and the Manic-Depressive—so get ready for Bachelor Number One.

The Game Player

CAN YOU TAKE IT?

If you like a challenge, somebody you can't figure out and control by the second date, give me a call and let's match wits, arm wrestle each other to the ground and may the best man win.

A Game Player will sit behind his eyes and watch you wander through the minefield all by yourself. This is a guy who will artificially create obstacles and tests for you, so you're going to feel as if you're always trying to prove yourself. He'll make himself sound like the Second Coming, telling you how cultured, wealthy, beloved, attractive, traveled, educated, loving, and terrific he is. You may wonder why he's alone, but he'll just tell you that he hasn't found the woman who can hold a candle to him.

This guy may be very appealing because he seems to have a lot of confidence, but he loves the in and out, the approach and avoidance—and what's really motivating him here is his own self-loathing. The closer you get to him, the greater his fear of exposure becomes, but he does love the game for the power and control it gives him, which compensates for his feelings of inadequacy. This is why he brags about himself to such an extent.

Unfortunately, this next dude doesn't have so much to crow about.

The Addict

> ## LOOKING FOR A NEW RUSH
> I used to jump outta perfectly good airplanes. After that I was the medic in the back of the helicopters with the big red target on the door. I want a woman who will drink with me, smoke with me and is not old baggage and doesn't need a bucket of pills to be happy, who'll keep me on the straight and narrow.

The Addict will use his addiction as part of the game, and the practice of hiding his issues makes him a Dance-Away Lover. He'll say, "Help me. I need you. You're the one who's going to save me from addiction. You're going to save me from gambling or pornography or drugs or drinking. You're going to be my angel." This is a very seductive dance because it makes you feel important. The Addict offers you great hope—and there's nothing more seductive in a relationship than that.

The problem is that when the relationship crashes, which it will, it's always going to be your fault. And not only is it your fault, but the Addict will then use whatever the addiction is as a way of dancing away from you and making you the warden, the mom, and the conscience by trying to hide it all, increasing the distance between you and him. Then the horrible cycle will begin: You'll try to save him, but there will be such self-loathing on his part that he'll say things like, "I don't know why you stay with me—you deserve somebody better. I'll understand if you want to leave." (He may even threaten suicide.) He's really putting the bait out there for you to either tell him you'll never leave no matter what *(Gotcha!),* or he's giving you permission to go: "See, I knew all along you'd leave me" *(Gotcha!* part II). It's heads he wins, tails you lose.

The cycle becomes uncomfortable and endless—and the only way to end it and avert disaster is to say: "I love and care for you, but you have to deal with this on your own. Your sobriety—and your sanity—has to be more important than us right now because there can be no us until you're clean and sober [or not gambling or whatever]. When you've been sane and cool for a year, call me, and we'll see if we can rebuild our relationship."

I know it's almost as difficult for you to give up your addiction to the situation and to him as it is for him to change his behavior because you've gotten seduced into it as much as he has. However, yours is a mere psychological addiction, while his is psychological plus biochemical, financial, or sexual. You're not doing yourself (or him) any favors by staying with somebody who's addicted because your presence can serve as a buffer, a distraction, or an excuse to continue the behavior. In other words, his addiction becomes your problem, and he won't take any responsibility for it as long as you're around.

~~~ ~~~

Since we're focusing on making yourself miserable in a relationship, you might be interested in the term *dysfunctional family.* This phrase was initially coined by social scientists who were studying alcoholic families years ago in an attempt to explain the somewhat unexpected phenomenon of the disintegration that occurred when the alcoholic in the family finally stopped drinking (a situation devoutly hoped and prayed for by everyone involved). The family structure was not only *not* strengthened, but it also quite often deteriorated completely, presumably because everything had previously circulated around the addict for so long that when the addiction went away, everybody felt either angry ("Gee, if you could do it now, why not when I asked you earlier?") or no longer morally superior to the alcoholic ("You could have done it before" or "I'm no use to you anymore").

Another explanation for the family's structural damage is that while the addiction was disastrous, the lack of it meant that family's center, or its defining principle, no longer existed. This means that if you stay with the Addict hoping to change or save him, then even if he does stop his destructive behavior, your prognosis as a couple is dismal. This is good news if you're looking for a lifetime of misery; otherwise, for both of your sakes, walking away sooner instead of later is the only hope for either of you.

Recently, researchers discovered that *sober* or *dry alcoholics* (that is, individuals who define themselves as alcoholics but are no longer actively drinking) have a rate of depression that's ten times higher than the population at large. This assumes that these people aren't depressed because they stopped drinking, but they started drinking because they were depressed.

One of the things that we know about drugs is that they work: If you're unhappy with your life and who you are, drinking is a way of not dealing with your problems (at least temporarily), of both tolerating yourself when you're drinking and hating yourself for drinking when you're sober—in other words, of being a Dance-Away Lover with yourself.

The Manic-Depressive

NOT YOUR AVERAGE GUY

I have bursts of energy and then need some quiet time alone. I can be entertaining once I've recharged my batteries. I'm serious minded but looking for someone who can teach me to have fun, but also respects my silences.

As opposed to the Addict, who's dealing with external chemical substances, the Manic-Depressive has little control over the chemical imbalances within himself. It's critical to understand the distinction between bipolar depression in contrast to simple unipolar depression: Depressives are sad, inert, and antisocial by and large, while the Manic-Depressive is capable of being a Dance-Away Lover. In his manic phase, the Manic-Depressive is charming, adorable, happy, and loads of fun. He has lots of energy, is very romantic and involved, wishes to spend gobs of time with you, and has grandiose plans for your future together. This is the guy who wants to marry you by the third date—in fact, he's already designed your dream house and matching wedding bands. According to him, sex has never been like this before; you've uncovered new erogenous zones in him. Everything is fabulous, fizzy, fantastic, seductive, sexy, and sensational . . . as long as he's in his mania.

Once he cycles into depression, however, everything bottoms out. He wants to be alone and has no time for you, and it's all your fault. You make him feel small and trapped, and you're mean if you don't understand his needs. The change is abrupt enough to be teeth rattling, a switch that turns on and off without warning. You can't trust his down moods (which may, in fact, become suicidal) any more than you can trust his up moods—but the real tragedy is that he can't trust them either. You're *both* being taken on an out-of-control merry-go-round with jarring, dissonant music and carousel horses constantly going up and down and leaping down off their platform. This guy is a prescription for misery, since trust is impossible: He'll never trust you because he can't trust himself. His emotional roller coaster will overpower any concerns for your well-being. His solicitousness will last only as long as his mania, and even then it will be tempered by his fascination with his own glee.

While his depressive episodes may scare the daylights out of both of you, professional intervention is tricky because so is the diagnosis. Even more important, the Manic-Depressive isn't chemically resistant to treatment, but he's often *emotionally* resistant—because while both of you hate the depressive phases, both of you really love the mania.

An untreated Manic-Depressive represents the same dilemma as the Addict: Stabilization takes time and effort, both of which are hard to come by in the early phases of dating. You have to not only spot the problem, but you also have to be willing to tell him: "Your sanity is more important than our relationship. And you have to be able to trust yourself before I can trust you." For both the Addict and the Manic-Depressive, the road to ruin is paved with a sign that doesn't warn YIELD, STOP, or CAUTION: SLIPPERY. Instead, you must say, "Go and get thee stabilized, and then call me. I care about you, but you have to care about yourself first."

And speaking of caring, the tricky parts are not only whom to care about and how to care, but also making sure that you're not taking over the caring role of someone completely inappropriate *and* inappropriately. While it's a common model for women to treat their menfolk like little boys, being a mom to an adult is an incredibly unsexy role. The next chapter explains what I mean.

CHAPTER 3
A Decalogue of Dunces

This chapter is a grab bag of the best of the rest of our disastrous dudes, beginning with that all-time winner, the poster boy of dunces.

The Mama's Boy

CHILD SEEKS MOTHER

After so many years alone, I'm a bit afraid of a relationship. Who will give a helping hand? The woman I would like to meet should be secure, not afraid to open up while having intelligence at her side at all times. If you're looking for a real man that is not a wimp and turns to jelly over good looks and looks for real substance behind the makeup, look no further. I want a woman who wants to take care of her man cause I do take care of someone I care about. Must want children. Must believe in family. Strong with me yet hold me when I need her to. Not bitter at men because of your past relationships.

Guys who are housebroken; know how to cook, clean, sew, and groom themselves; have acceptable manners; can recognize dirty from clean clothes; and are courteous and gentlemanly are certainly not to be sniffed at . . . assuming that they aren't so well brought up by Mama that leaving her isn't an option. If he's over 40 with no job and lives with his mother, he'll tell you that it's to take care of her, but you can bet that *she's* really taking care of *him*. While I know older women and younger men are all the rage now—there's even a term for it called *tadpoling*—guys who go after a "mature" woman may be thinking, *Mommy! She's mature, so I can be immature.*

You might expect Mama's Boys to be well dressed because of the female influence in their lives, but this isn't necessarily true. They can look very much like somebody who wants to be taken care of. On some level, they want you to be the mother with whom they feel involved because you can provide something that Mom can't: sexuality.

A Mama's Boy can be very seductive because he can really talk the talk. He's been raised by a woman and is seemingly very respectful of females in a society that's as chauvinistic as ours. The notion that somehow this guy is respectful of your intelligence, independence, brains, personality, and career can seem very appealing. He'll seem to idolize, respect, and adore you—he'll practically make a religion of you, the blessed female. And guess who the role model for this larger-than-life woman is? Yep, you got it . . . Mom.

As you may expect, he'll expect you to take a motherly role in the relationship—indulging, applauding, nurturing, and chasing after him, all the while telling him that you love him. Even in the midst of an argument, he'll want you to comfort him and give him a cookie. He'll act like a denied little child whenever he thinks he's not getting enough attention. And he never feels the need to apologize—ever. If you have the audacity to get angry with him, he'll just look confused and mutter, "But I love you." This is his way of erasing the slate.

The Mama's Boy will never negotiate with you because he considers himself completely powerless, and the more powerless he feels, the more likely he is to strike out at you by any means at his disposal. He views his behavior as boyishly naughty rather than destructive because you're the female authority figure, while he's merely the little kid. (The mental image is of the small child madly windmilling his arms futilely against a big, giggly parent who's untouched because her hand is on his forehead, thus keeping him at arm's length.)

It's likely that the Mama's Boy will tell you all about his wonderful mother on your first date, which you may find charming. But no matter what he tells you, this man has an ambivalent relationship with his mother. We live in a society in which children are primarily raised by women, no matter how often we hear stories about John Lennon or "Mr. Mom". Now, when a two-year-old begins that first lurch toward independence, a little girl has a relatively easy job of it: That is, she can dress in her mother's clothes and scold her dollies and therefore manage independence by both identifying with and moving away from her mother, which allows her to define her own personality.

On the other hand, the male at two has a much more complicated task because the normal push away from his mother is complicated by the fact that if he starts wearing her clothes or talking like her, he'll be made fun of. (Being called a Mama's Boy is the ultimate insult in our society.) His father at this point is a much more distant figure, so when the little boy is feeling lonely, sad, or needy, his wanting to be close to Mom, but also feeling compromised and less "manly" because of it, makes his identity shakier. The dilemma becomes how to feel close to, but not engulfed by, Mom.

Closeness to this important first woman is basic and threatening at the same time, and it can set up a lifelong tension of both being desperate for, and terrified of, closeness with this woman . . . or any woman. Consequently, a man who hasn't sorted out his relationship with his mother is poison because it means that he hasn't sorted out his anger—the source of which is the conflict between his longing for, and terror of, emotional and physical intimacy. He'll love and hate you for the same behavior: He'll be both attracted and repelled by your strength and decisiveness, charmed and threatened by your intelligence, and publicly proud of your success while privately accusing you of competing with and castrating him.

The Mama's Boy may behave like the Dance-Away Lover once you get close to him. Something that you view as a positive experience will cause him to walk away because his sense of intimacy is still entangled with the confusion about wanting to be close to a female, yet he's terrorized by the thought of losing his sense of himself as a man.

The polar opposite of the Mama's Boy is a guy who's somehow resolved his issues with both his mother *and* his father, realizing that they're individuals instead of the icons he saw them as a child. He somehow has an adult connection with both parents as opposed to a relationship with only one, or an angry or overly involved relationship with either. He understands that before they were "Mom" and "Dad," they had first names.

The Passive-Aggressive

LONELY MAN WANTS TO FIND LOVE

I usually get into trouble thinking about someone else instead of myself. I am not selfish, just the opposite. I tend to give and never expect anything in return. Life is what you put into it. You have to make a deposit before you make a withdrawal. I'm a very lonely man and tired of head games. I'm very romantic and I know how to treat women right. I don't cheat or lie to women and I don't care about how the woman looks. It's inside that counts and I have a good paying job. If you are looking for a man that will treat you like a queen like you should be treated, I know I'm not that handsome but I'm very sweet, caring and romantic. . . .

I'm looking for women to treat me like a prince or a king cause I treat girls like the best and I'm looking for a girl that don't cheat. Age or looks does not matter at all. I am tired of all the games that are being played from these women I tend to meet. Where are all the nice, down to earth ones? I believe in being honest and sincere. I am close to my family and enjoy the holidays around them. I would like to find someone who I can be open with, someone I can talk to openly, someone I can share even the simplest little things. Maybe I am asking way too much here, but it's always worth a shot.

Run! Danger: Passive-Aggressive alert! If you met this dude at the Laundromat, he might offer you a quarter; at a movie theater, he'd let you get ahead of him in the popcorn line, but his seeming good manners barely hide his fury, reminding you of the following joke: How many Passive-Aggressives does it take to change a lightbulb? Well, none: "It's okay. You go ahead and take the lightbulb. I'll just sit in the dark and worry about it without you." (Of course, if you've ever dealt with a true Passive-Agressive, I guess I won't hear you laughing. . . .)

A Passive-Aggressive will say, "My friends tell me I'm handsome and good company, and they can't understand why I haven't found the perfect woman," or "Well, when I talked to my friends about this, they said you shouldn't do this." He feels anger just like everyone else but believes on some level that expressing that anger would be dangerous, so his so-called passivity makes him safe by forcing *you* to act.

This guy won't ever boast about anything, which you may find charmingly humble, but understand that he also won't claim any of his anger, laziness, or sadness either. If you haven't figured this out already, this means that everything—*ta-dah!*—is going to be your fault. If you try to force him to take responsibility for his behavior, he's going to dodge you like a silver bullet. He'll say, "Right. It's all my fault. Everything is always my fault," which is just another way of saying, "It's never my fault." So, instead of his claiming his feelings with a "Look, I'm angry with you!" or "Why can't we talk about this?" it's always going to be anyone else's fault but his.

If you're looking for visual cues from this dude, body language can often be a tip-off. Passive-Aggressives are so unused to dealing with their anger that they often hunch over or won't make eye contact with you. So, if your guy's arms are crossed across his chest at all times—bingo! You've found Mr. Passive Aggressive! How lucky can one gal be?

The Whiner

PATHETIC DORK SEEKS HOTTIE???

Alright, I've had an ad for almost a month now and have had ZERO success. As if it isn't already awkward enough meeting people this way, I have to have my confidence crushed by every other girl that I contact. Ladies, please tell me what I'm doing wrong here? I thought I was a pretty good catch until getting shot down by almost every girl on this site. I know, a picture would help, but I'm a little bit shy about posting one for all to see. I really doubt I will find the lady of my dreams here, but you never know. I am just sick of the long nights alone when I know there are ladies out there with the same problem. Just looking for someone to care about who will also care about me. Not looking for Miss Perfect, after all none of us are perfect. I am just not looking forward to another long cold New York winter with only my cats for company. I am the kind of guy who enjoys nights at home in front of the TV, watching a good movie. I am also hoping to find someone else who is an animal lover as I have owned cats for years (well, maybe they own me, but that's another story).

Now, I don't know who would respond to that ad, but obviously, this guy thought that it would work . . . and there's no reason to believe that he doesn't present himself in real life exactly the same way. Most of us know people who declare, "Well, you probably wouldn't go out with somebody like me," or "Gee, most women are pretty mean, but you look like somebody who wouldn't stomp on me like the other women I've dated." This is the same person who stood up in school and said, "This is probably a stupid question, but . . ." Look, if it's stupid, why ask it? And if it's worth asking, then step up, take your chances, and don't ask other people to affirm your right to exist.

My mama always told me that lifelong bachelors were that way for a reason. These days, both men and women wait longer to marry, but I'd still be really cautious with anybody over 40 who, when asked why he's not married, smiles shyly and then goes into his Average Joe rant: "I'm just a simple man with a good job and a decent personality. I was in love only once a long time ago, and it made me gun-shy for a long time." His frustrations and anger will then slowly bubble to the surface: "I have no type in women. I don't care if she's a little taller or makes more money than me. I'm looking for someone I can talk to. I hate games, and I won't play them. Period."

These guys are everywhere. You can find them online, and you can find them in life. They're the dudes who won't make eye contact with you, but they'll come and find you, for they have an extraordinary amount of willingness to put themselves out there, but they make a science of feeling good about feeling bad, thus playing on your sympathy. And they may be very attractive to you if you've just been with a flirt or a cheater because they're able to resonate with that part of you that doesn't feel very happy about yourself. You'll think, *This is great. I don't have to worry about him going after some other woman. Because he's so needy, I'll provide what he needs, and then he'll never leave me.*

There's a wonderful short story by Anne Tyler about a woman who was married to an attractive philanderer. Over the years, she caught him in numerous affairs, yet every night she'd pray that he'd view her as the most important person in his life, that he'd be unaware of other women, that his face would light up every time she walked in the room, and that he'd spend every waking hour thinking about her. Well, eventually her husband had a stroke and lost all but his short-term memory. He couldn't remember anybody or anything and became housebound, and she became the only person in his life. Well, she got her wish, but she never imagined how incredibly restrictive it would be.

So even if your fantasy that this guy will never leave you turns out to be true (which it won't), you need to be careful what you wish for. Even though he may bring out the Florence Nightingale or the social worker in you, my suggestion is to run for the hills. No matter what you do, the Whiner is going to be miserable.

Regardless of how he really feels, if you ask, "How do you feel today?" he'll always tell you that he's sick. If you ask how things are going at work, he'll unfailingly say how horribly they went. But understand that he won't be the least bit tolerant of any of the unhappiness or unpleasantness in your life. *He* wants to be the primary sad person—so the possibility of making this guy happy is . . . slim to none. He may need medication, he may need therapy, but he doesn't need you.

The Control Freak

NOT INTERESTED IN PLAYING GAMES

Well first off, I don't play games. I am looking for someone that is beyond the game playing stages. I don't have time for that nonsense anymore. I would like to find someone who is stable (emotionally and financially). Please don't contact me if you have a lot of baggage or unresolved issues from past relationships. I hope to find someone that can be my best friend, and who will grow into a loving, honest, caring relationship. I am a very straightforward person. I believe if two people are attracted to each other there is no reason to beat around the bush. I like just picking up and going somewhere new on weekends, so you must be willing to do the same.

She must have personal goals for herself, and is going to go through with them. Someone that loves to be around her man, but also knows how to give just the right amount of space so we both can breathe. Someone who will share in my likes and interests. My life is pretty much set. I've got a good secured job, I have a 3 bedroom 2 bath home nestled in the wooded cove by a river. I own three autos. I'm not going to write a novel here but I'm interested in finding a good quality female to be friends with and go from there. Please, make sure your emotional problems from something that happened to you in the past is a million miles behind you before contacting me. I can only be your boyfriend, not your psychologist.

To explain the contrast between his physiognomy and his success with women, Henry Kissinger once famously said that power is an aphrodisiac. The line between power and control can get a bit confusing when that macho dude you meet on the singles cruise tells you up front that he's sometimes hard to deal with but worth every minute. "I set the standards!" he proclaims, beating his chest. "I'm highly capable of anything. You want spontaneity—done. Ambition—done. Intelligence—done. Motivation—done. Soul—done. I encompass every realm of man that man can encompass. Period."

Wow, heady stuff, even if you think he's kidding. This guy will definitely have a certain sparkle, dines well, smiles charmingly, and will come across as more handsome than he really is. His stock in trade is his confidence: "If I want something, I can get it. There really are no barriers in life, only *perceptions* of barriers. I'm visionary and resourceful, and one hell of a lot of fun—if I decide to be."

He'll tell you that he's been looking for you his whole life, that he's dated lots of women because he was unwilling to "settle." (What do you suppose he told all those other women?!) He'll say that he's looking for a woman who can take charge at times, but what he really means is that he'd like to find someone who's got his back and who's open to trying new things. He'll emphasize that you've got to take care of yourself (physically) so that you can take care of him (sexually).

He'll regale you with tales of how successful and accomplished he is, and say that he's comfortable in pinstripes but is really a jeans-and-loafers type at heart. And speaking of heart, he won't be shy about mentioning his philanthropy, as well as his financial commitments. But now that he's ready for you, he's willing to swap business time for a personal life. He'll want you to abandon your own pursuits to suit his because he wants you available to him 24/7/365 (unless he wants time with his interests). Oh, and did I forget to mention that he'd also like a family? That means the equation is: me, rich Tarzan; you, young, fertile, pliable Jane.

As you can see, as opposed to some other types, the Control Freak will tell you a fair amount of detail about himself—but that's not the tip-off. That will come later on, when he starts to make rules for you. He'll be very specific about when he's available for you and under what circumstances, and he'll certainly pick the places you go. None of this is necessarily bad, but if you somehow can't meet one of his conditions, it's very likely that he'll drop you. He allows absolutely no ambiguity, no negotiation, and no mediation. It's his way or the highway. Now, in adult dating it's not unusual for both parties to be used to having their own way—the question is, to what extent are you willing to go to ensure your way, and how angry are you going to be if your wishes are thwarted?

If you're uncertain about whether your new friend is caring or controlling, you can inject a little ambiguity in the situation. Now I'm not a great believer in playing games, but if you find yourself trying desperately to please this man to no avail, then you need to at least entertain the possibility of trying to do something your way in order to see what his reaction will be. If he's willing to negotiate with you, then you've misdiagnosed him. If he's not, *bingo!* You're dating Mr. It's All about Me!

(One little postscript here: Control Freaks may very well be meticulous and obsessive about their dress; however, they're just as likely to be somewhat sloppy because their need to control a situation is really a statement of inner chaos and insecurity. If they don't completely have command of a situation, they fear that it will get away from them and they'll be exposed as fraudulent, incapable, or incompetent. So don't buy into the "Oscar = slob, Felix = neat freak" school of haberdashery.)

The Misogynist

LOOKING FOR A REAL WOMAN

I will make you laugh, and even cry a little. I am blunt and to the point. I can smell a liar from a mile away. I work hard, and have goals. I am a real as they come. Please no negative persons, non-serious types, non-emotional types, or materialistic divas. Save that for the rap moguls. I hold my own, but don't need the drama. So I prefer straight-forward, real, and normal. I have to say if you are totally shy, a liar, don't have pictures to back up your claims, want to speak 5 years on the phone before meeting, or live over 50 miles from me, don't have time to call, or write back within reason. Don't respond. Can't hold a conversation with criticism? Don't need you. Believe me when I say people are weird. Some get to different stages . . . like we actually meet, and then they have a change of heart. That's because they are confused. Hopefully you won't be a B.S.er and waste my time with your email. Since after all I paid my money. Some have read this and still don't understand. Read it over 3X. Say a prayer, see a shrink, get a hug, sit in a bubble bath for a few and ponder. If you are secure then holla at me.

OBNOXIOUS, SMART-ASSED, EMOTIONALLY CRIPPLED SEX-ADDICT SEEKS SAME

Insane, secretly famous, disgusted hipster. I'm one of those classic guys with the damaged checkered past and a heart of gold, and apparently hot. So why am I single, you ask? Because I attract women who are damaged goods, mainly because I carry a little of that aura myself. I scare most women who *aren't* walking wounded before they get a chance to know me. . . .

I'm not in a situation or location where there are many women with whom I'm going to have *anything* in common with, culturally or otherwise. I spend lots of time outdoors—for example, hiking around for two weeks in remote areas of canyonlands is my idea of fun, I just don't do it augmented by hallucinogens anymore—that often, anyway. I rock-climb, ski, love guns and kids (I only belong to two organizations—the NRA and the ACLU), spend a lot of time with books, have encyclopedic knowledge of obscure post-marxist theory among other stuff, have a couple books in print, used to publish a magazine and worked at a famous one as an editor, used to run an art gallery, I am only satisfied sexually if it's happening at least thrice daily. I love women. I hate anything that smacks of manipulation, dissembling, or whining. Say something other than what you mean and I will evaporate. Seeking a Punk-rock/hippie earth-momma who disdains makeup and loves freedom, who may've at some point morphed into a tack-sharp academic. In other words, no dummy.

Physically/psychically active. Willing to try almost anything once—*has* tried almost anything once. Doesn't plan on "settling down", but plans on having a life that is stable enough and independent enough to build a support structure for continued adventures—and having *that* be stability and being settled. Wants a *partner*—not someone to take care of or to take care of her. Any woman who identifies with/talks about television—particularly "the bachelor/bachelorette"—need not apply. If you love/live for money and shiny things, stay away. Consumer society creates soulless, cowering prostitutes who can find solace only in entertainment and consumption . . . not interested in mating with a slave (or a whore, which is just a slave with the illusion of control). You've gotta be funny, and not as serious as I'm sounding here (I'm not either).

(**Author's note:** *I think this guy used asterisks in an attempt to show that he's witty—or facetious or sarcastic. Or maybe he's just trying to emphasize a few things. I'm reproducing his ad verbatim, including asterisks, so you decide.*)

What more can I say? These guys are both classic misogynists (I had to include 'em both so that you wouldn't believe either was unique). Now, a *misogynist* by definition is someone who hates females—even though you'll hear him say, "I love women." (Now, to say that you love women is about as sensible as saying that you hate women. You like different characteristics of people, but saying that you love all women is like saying, "Some of my best friends are black, Puerto Rican, Jewish, or Chinese." People are who they are.) Men who adamantly proclaim their adoration for the fairer sex quite often don't love us at all. They love the sexuality of women, being in control of women, or what women can do for them. They aren't capable of friendship with women or equality in their relationships. What they want is someone to dominate.

The Misogynist is a man who finds fault with you all the time, tells you that that's not how a feminine or liberated woman would act, points out what your place is in this life, and claims that if God had meant for women to be equals, He would have made them so. All these things may seem adorable and appealing because it may make you feel very feminine. In other words, a man who opens a door for you can be either polite or a woman hater, and it's very hard to differentiate.

I'm not saying that you should open your own doors, but if there's any question in your mind as to whether or not this man really does treat you as an equal, know that the Misogynist is quite often a bigot in other areas of his life, too: He makes fun of gays; he's rude to waiters or waitresses, secretaries, salesclerks, busboys, and cab drivers; and he's demeaning to people who seemingly have less status than he does. The Misogynist will comment on your femininity, tell you not to "worry your pretty little head about this," and tell you that you're cute when you're angry. And you'll never win an argument because he'll ignore your points.

The Misogynist won't view you as an equal, but will place you on a pedestal . . . and that's somebody who basically doesn't like women. Quite often, if you scratch this character deep enough, you'll find a very insecure man who feels that his only way of having the ability to not only dominate but to have any importance in this world is to lord himself over inferiors, the weaker sex, the little woman.

The Competitor

SEEKING STRONG, INDEPENDENT WOMAN
I've never understood why a woman who could flex a muscle, use her mind, express her feelings, communicate and be passionate would be considered a threat or intimidating.

(**Author's note:** *And why, pray tell, did these thoughts come to mind if we're not Mr. Competitive?*)

At first blush, the Competitor may look like a very liberated man. He appears to be a guy who respects women and is challenged by intellectual pursuits, which makes him look initially like the perfect catch for a career-minded gal who's always secretly felt that her femininity is compromised by her intelligence, success, or education. He seems to truly want what a lot of smart, accomplished women desire: a partner. The basic underlying philosophy of the Competitor is that on some level he really *does* want somebody who can give him a run for his money. He'd rather play tennis with somebody who plays well, and he'd rather do a crossword puzzle with someone who has an extensive vocabulary.

He likes the fact that you're not only interested in things he's good at, but you excel at them, too—and your tendency will be to let go of your reticence to beat a man, which is advice that mothers have passed on to daughters for ages. ("Never beat a man; if anything, make him feel important.") Because he seems to really relish your abilities, you may let go of that sensitivity to the fact that beating a man at his own game isn't a good idea. Beware: This is a guy who likes to raise the bar—as long as he can still get over it first and best and always.

Should you ever best him at something, you're going to have a real problem on your hands. What you'll find is that he's incredibly charming when he does win . . . but when he loses, he'll be in a funk for so long that you'll want to pick another sport. This isn't only because he's the Competitor; it's because he's a male who's grown up in a society in which men are taught that winning is all—everything else is just excuses. So when you beat him, it will blindside you both because he'll be as surprised at his fury at you as you'll be, and both of you will feel that you've been conned.

He'll withhold sex, which is something that women have traditionally done to manipulate men, but men can do it as well. And although the Competitor can become instantly unavailable, he isn't like the Dance-Away Lover; instead, he's simply somebody who needs to win. Even early on, if you're just playing Monopoly, he *must* be the victor. So unless you want to go through your life losing to this guy all the time, the two of you need to sort this out early on. The easiest way of dealing with the Competitor is to just refuse to play.

Another concern with this guy is what happens when you make more money than he does (and keep in mind that 30 percent of all women are now making more than their husbands): Again, the Competitor will be very proud of you if you're making a good living . . . as long as he's making more. So the first time you bring home a bigger paycheck, you may find your relationship in serious jeopardy.

The Narcissist

SHINE ON ME

I have a dazzling personality. I'm a natural leader. I'm smart, insightful. I do what I say and say what I mean, very attractive and masculine qualities. I've always had lots of friends. I bring more time, understanding, and support to friendships than most men. I also have an emotional depth that most men lack. In fact, I'm ready and able at this point in my life to experience romance and a powerful "spark" with someone special. I'm a pillar of strength. I'm successful in my career. People can rely on me. I'm an independent guy, not someone who "wears his heart on his sleeve" so even those closest to me don't always know how I feel. But my masculine and stable presence in life makes me worth the investment to get to know. I'm handsome, 5'11" tall, 175 lbs, beautiful physique, muscular and athletic and in excellent health. Still have a good mop of hair, nice teeth and beautiful, beautiful eyes.

I'm looking for a very balanced woman. She'll have clear goals in life and dreams she hopes to pursue. She'll constantly be juggling things in her life but will still find a place for me. Women who are truly balanced like this are rare, but they do exist. We will share a number of positive qualities, including: She's really easy to get along with and won't boss me around. She has her eye on the future and has big goals and dreams for what she wants out of life.

While insecurity is seldom appealing, our competitive society seems to bring out the wimp in a lot of guys when it comes to dating—so a man who seems sure of himself can look mighty good. This dude might describe himself over a quiet candlelit dinner as kind, loving, compassionate, passionate, open-minded, creative, and successful. He might be quite serious as he goes on to detail his philosophic, scientific, spiritual, and psychological sides, telling you how much he enjoys stimulating and interesting conversations as well as open and intimate sharing. Just when you think he's going to take a breath and ask something—anything—about you, he'll tell you how much he loves his work while also having many diverse interests: a variety of outdoor sports, music of many types, dance, theater, good food, reading, and so on.

He'll then explain how he's really looking for an intense, loving connection as well as space for his interests and downtime for personal restoration. Lest you may not have noticed, he'll remind you that he's youthful in mind, spirit, and body (which is pretty much the same size and shape as when he was 18), and that "people" have always told him how good-looking he is.

You'll think, *Wow, isn't it nice to be around a guy who's so confident,* but it may occur to you that if this guy's so fantastic, why isn't he in a relationship? Well, he's already told you—he loves himself, and there's not enough room in his little pea-picking heart for both him and someone else. Understand very early on that this guy will never pass a mirror without checking himself out. When you actually meet him, he may be surprisingly ordinary looking, but that doesn't affect his perception of himself. He's convinced that the entire world is revolving slowly, and solely, around him.

Now the reason he got that way is because he was the only son of a single mother, the oldest in a family of women (sisters and a single mom), or an only child. In his adult world, regardless of his background, he's the "only"—which means that he's not going to have a whole lot of room for you. The relationship will work only if you're completely willing to take a backseat and see yourself as a groupie or supporting character.

If your self-description is: "I want to be an audience; I want to bask in somebody else's glow; I don't want to have to put myself out in a relationship," then you've found the perfect guy because he'll never ask you what you think of anybody but him. He'll tell you about his day, his workout, his friends, his successes, and he may even be willing to tell you about his failures—but they really aren't failures; they're the result of other people being unable to appreciate him.

Telltale signs are there for the noticing if you think you may be dating the Narcissist: You've probably noticed your bruises from being elbowed out of the way every time you tried to reapply your lipstick in front of a mirror, and his styling products take up much more room in the bathroom than yours—whether he has hair or not. Finally, if there's any doubt in your mind, tell him that you've had a bad day and need him to listen to you so that you can vent for a while—if he truly belongs in this category, he'll either be busy, put you off, fidget, take over the conversation, or change the subject. The Narcissist cares about you and your opinion only as it relates to him.

The Trust-Fund Kid

HEART OF GOLD

I've been to the best schools, come from the best family, spend summers in Newport, am fluent in several languages. Looking for a woman with a heart of gold who comes from a similar background. Must look good in yachting whites and know how to handle herself in all circumstances, be it curtseying before the queen or dealing with servants.

The Trust-Fund Kid is someone who assumes that nobody would want him except for his money, so he's going to be hostile about everything. He'll be the chintziest guy you've ever met in your life: He's perfectly willing to take you out on the family yacht, but he's going to make you take the train to get there by yourself, and he'll make you take a taxi to the house. He may dress very poorly, and he'll never offer to buy you anything or pay for very much—and when he does take you out, it will be Bargain Basement all the way.

This is a guy who really feels that no one would love him if it weren't for his family. He might very well be haunted by the "stupid grandson theory of life," which was developed as an economic theory to underscore investment strategies, but it applies to dating as well. This theory acknowledges that most geniuses don't become recognized or successful until the middle or latter part of their lives. So if you could invest with a genius, by the time you found him, he'd be in his 40s, and if you were very lucky, you'd make a lot of money with him.

The genius's son grew up with a distracted and often absent father, who wasn't there because he was always off doing other things (such as making the family name and fortune). Now, if this son of a genius has been handed his father's company, it won't make the scads of money that would have accrued from investing with the father—but the son won't lose your principal either, because he's well aware of his deficiencies as compared to Dad. Consequently, he'll be careful, trying to maintain what his father accomplished.

The third generation—the grandson of a genius—is an investment disaster. He's two generations removed from genius, grew up with privilege, compared his father with his grandfather and found his father wanting, and has neither the genius of his grandfather nor the conservative nature and intimidation of his father, so he'll run a company into the ground.

The idea here is that the Trust-Fund Kid didn't make the money, so he doesn't feel a sense of accomplishment. He grew up with privilege and feels inadequate because he thinks he could never earn it on his own. He'll feel that he's a part of the "Groucho Marx school of life" (often mistakenly attributed to Woody Allen), which is "I don't care to belong to any club that will have me as a member." Therefore, he'll go out of his way to be tightfisted and fairly hostile. And the fact that TV shows such as *Joe Millionaire* and *Who Wants to Marry a Millionaire?* have made Americans believe that every woman, especially the pretty, telegenic ones, are only after a man for his money is only making this worse.

The Gold Digger

ACTOR SEEKING INDEPENDENT WOMAN
Actor interested in female who likes soap operas! Looking for employed female such as a doctor who would like to meet an attractive single male who likes soap operas.

As girls, most of us were exposed to the notion that an unscrupulous woman might use her feminine wiles to pursue a man based on his wallet size. Well, I'm here to tell you that the notion that gold diggers only come in pink is a mistaken one.

The (male) Gold Digger is undoubtedly attractive and will describe himself as a model or an actor; he'll tell you about how often he works out; and he'll probably be very well dressed. He'll tell you that he has a tux and is available to be your escort anyplace you want to go. He'll also mention very early on that he makes a relatively modest income as a carpenter or some other kind of blue-collar job, but he's not at all threatened by your income or your career.

This is a guy who's used to being arm candy. When the two of you go places together, he'll explain that going dutch will allow the two of you to date a lot more . . . but you'll end up paying the bills. He'll conveniently leave his wallet behind; or if the two of you go shopping, he'll happily allow you to buy him anything your little heart desires.

Understand that the Gold Digger will view himself as essentially a male bimbo. If that's what you want, fine, but be aware of it. His appeal is that he's not only *not* threatened by your wealth and power, he's turned on by it because he views you as a valuable resource. If you want the power that being a sugar mommy implies, then this is the guy for you.

The Self-Loather

LONESOME & LOOKING

I was always picked last in Red Rover, I always seem to be in the wrong hemisphere. The result is a wacky ball of seeming contradictions that are well known to those who can tolerate me. If your social life has gone from bad to worse lately, and the silence creeps up on you when your telephone rings— we have a lot on common.

Our society breeds self-loathers. While we give lots of space to the notion that women who hate themselves get into abusive relationships with men, and men who hate themselves are Dance-Away Lovers, the question is this: Is it possible for either sex to avoid self-loathing? Because we live in a capitalist society, we all buy things that we don't need. Now, how do you create that artificial need? Well, you convince people that whatever they are is wrong. They smell wrong, look wrong, and act wrong. Their breasts are too small or too big; their legs are too long or too short; their hair is too straight or too curly; their eyes are too wide or too narrow. If they could only find the right beer, the right car, the right tie, or the right underwear, they'd be lovable. So to talk about self-loathing to a certain extent is a bit futile, since it really is the basis of the American character. Nevertheless, we need to both acknowledge it and take it into account.

Show me somebody who doesn't have low self-esteem, and I'll show you somebody who came from another country or galaxy far, far away. This means that a bit of insecurity is par for the course. The real questions are:

1. How truly insecure is this person?
2. How pathological is it?
3. How is it expressed?

Insecurity is never all that charming, but it's ubiquitous and certainly underlies all our characters. However, it can be understood, contained, and used positively, and you may even be able to tame your own demons, recognize them, and *voilà!*—find a nice guy who's not too insecure and balances rather than exacerbates your insecurities. That's right, cherubs, there *are* some good guys out there, and we'll learn all about them in the next chapter.

CHAPTER 4
The Good Guy

So a miracle has occurred: You've found a guy who isn't too good to be true, but is in fact a keeper. He's not perfect—you have arguments, and he may have a few tics that you're not crazy about—but the two of you are really looking at your relationship like Velcro, in the sense that you have enough points of contacts to stick together. You like to do some of the same kinds of things. You can talk to each other. The sex is good—it may not be the best either of you have ever had, but that may not be the most important thing (although since we're talking about romantic dating here, presumably there should be *some* sexual attraction).

Beware of finding either your soul mate or the person who "completes" you. Incomplete people need therapists, not dates. They attract and then aggravate the daylights out of one another: She initially thought he was the bubbly life of the party, but two years later she now knows that he's a big flirt who never pays any attention to her. Or she thinks that he's this solid guy who's trustworthy and could love no one but her . . . only to discover that he's a leech who's sucking all the blood out of her, and she can't get any time for herself.

As for soul mates—bah, humbug. Each of us has to be aware of and comfortable with our own identities. In other words, I'm not sure what a soul is, and I'm not sure how we know our souls, but if there is such a thing and it is knowable, we're *only* going to know our own. This means that when you call somebody else a soul mate, you're going to superimpose who you want him or her to be on who they actually are. Furthermore, the assumption of sameness leaves both parties incapable of negotiating the differences that will inevitably occur between two people. So if you're even thinking of using the term *soul mate* to describe your good guy, consider yourself slapped to the curb.

When you're talking about a person who's a good mate, you need to figure out the important criteria. For example, consider spirituality: If you're a very religious person, you may want to find someone who shares your beliefs—otherwise you're going to have arguments not only on Saturday and Sunday mornings, but also during the rest of the week as well.

Energy level is also an important consideration: If one of you has a lot of it, while the other has none, it may be really fun at the beginning. The high-energy person may entertain the low-energy person, and the low-energy person may calm the high-energy person. But in the long run, the high-energy person will always be going, leaving the low-energy person to feel like he's being dragged along.

Also, look at your views of money: If your guy's very extravagant, but you hold on to a nickel until it screams, he's initially going to be very impressed by what a good saver you are, but sooner or later he's going to view you as chintzy, and you're going to think of him as a spendthrift.

You don't have to have identical educational backgrounds, but if one person feels significantly smarter or better educated than the other, then sooner or later it's going to cause some problems. Similarly, I don't think that you have to be the same age, but if one person is significantly older than the other, you have to figure out the ramifications and long-term consequences (and you may want to reread the Control Freak and Mama's Boy sections).

Mr. Right

Okay, let's assume that you've found someone whom you genuinely like. We're not talking about opposites attracting, but we're also not talking about finding somebody who's your identical match—you're not complete opposites, you're not soul mates. This isn't a lust at first sight or a "Well, there's nobody else around here, so I may as well marry this person," kind of settling, desperation thing. The two of you have a lot to talk about, and you have more or less the same level of energy. You've spent enough time together, so you actually know how both of you behave. This is a guy who's been divorced for at least a year, has a reasonable relationship with his parents, and shares the same value system as you. He's interested in who you are, has the same need for both intimacy and distance that you do, and is willing to argue about things that are important. He likes your friends, and they like him. You enjoy lots of the same activities, you share the same spiritual commitment, and you make each other laugh.

Congratulations—you're actually in a relatively good relationship with one of the four remaining good guys still out there! However, a nondisastrous guy doesn't completely eliminate the possibility of dating disaster and pulled hair and torn garments, because you don't need him to make you miserable. You—yes, sweet li'l ol' you—can make your own catastrophe. Have no fear: I'll show you exactly how to do it! In the next section, I'll provide you with a step-by-step, easy-to-follow blueprint of how others just like you managed to blow seemingly well-grounded relationships sky-high. Take notes if you wish.

PART II

Doom-a-Date

CHAPTER 5
First Impressions

In the last section, you learned how to find your perfectly disastrous date, thereby ensuring a life of misery, but it's important to leave nothing to chance. You can also doom your dating life with your own behavior. Rather than finding a disastrous date, you can *be* one! This chapter will tell you how.

Let's Start at the Beginning . . .

Whether male or female, you only get one chance to make a first impression, and that chance is surprisingly fleeting. You aren't always going to be instantly aware when somebody's eyeballing you, but let's assume for a moment that you're indeed prepared for that two seconds when your intended falls hopelessly into your thrall.

When you catch a prime contender checking you out, lick your lips slowly and meaningfully, thereby instantly establishing yourself as definitely not from the land of the uptight. Staring at body parts, either his or yours—and touching yours to reaffirm that you actually have them—also ensures a great start. A salacious wink can't hurt either (I must admit that I'm terrible at winking because I always look like I'm having a seizure, but you should feel free to go for it). Guys, many of you have been practicing these techniques forever, but they can work disastrously for you women, too, so why be left out? But I digress. . . .

Next, you can gaze deeply into his eyes, forcing him to wimp out and break the stare first. Establish your dominance from the outset—which can only occur by invading his body space. Touch his shoulder or arm, and let your touch linger at least a heartbeat or two too long. If he's cold enough to try to keep you at arm's length by just shaking hands, you can either grab his elbow and move in, or simply don't let go of his hand. (Then there's always that cute little trick where you tickle his palm while shaking hands.)

Chewing gum is also a great way to make a first impression because the "cow chewing its cud" look is a reminder that we're all really animals. Winding your hair around your fingers or picking at yourself (toes, nose, zits, and scabs are all great choices) are also effective signals that indicate how unafraid you are of intimacy or being real. And if your ear happens to itch, just stick your finger right in there and see what you can dig out. After all, first impressions are so important!

Avoiding Disasters

Okay, you understand that I was being facetious—please tell me you did! But seriously, if you're trying not to doom-a-date, then your appearance should be friendly but relatively nonsexual (at least at the outset). I know, this is dating, which is inherently a sexual activity, but believe me, being overtly sexual from the get-go will give a man the feeling that since he's a stranger, you'd be sexual with anybody, which is more likely to turn him off rather than on—especially if he's looking for something other than a quickie. Men are still burdened by the suspicion that women believe that men are only interested in one thing, even in this day and age. So by being warm yet nonthreatening, and keeping your sexuality on low, you're much more inviting; consequently, you'll encourage someone to feel safe enough to get close to you, both literally and figuratively.

Eye contact, especially if it's easy, open, and not a penetrating stare, makes you seem both interesting and interested, confident but not controlling, and friendly rather than intimidating. Whether it's intentional or accidental, mirroring behavior—that is, crossing your legs if his are crossed, smiling when he smiles, leaning forward when he does, and so on—establishes a rhythm and a connection. As you find yourself feeling comfortable with this person, the two of you might even start breathing in tandem with one another, which is a very good sign.

While you may be interested in establishing a more tangible, physical connection, err on the side of safety and keep all physical contact to a minimum. I know the popular notion is that touching someone's arm or leg or moving the hair off their face means that you're establishing interest in them in a gentle way, but that's mostly Hollywood's take. A movie has to condense a relationship into a few scenes—you don't. So, in real life, staying within your personal space and allowing the other person to do the same initially gives you both a feeling of comfort and safety.

If you wait to invade a man's body space until you've been invited to do so, it will feel welcoming to you both, rather than like an assault. The invitation can be made in a number of ways that are reflected in posture, stance, gesture, or expression, all of which is commonly known as *body language*. If your date-to-be has his arms crossed over his chest, his legs stiff, and/or his knees and thighs clutched together so tightly that they could keep a dime from falling—back off. If his posture reminds you of a turtle pulling in its head and limbs to the smallest possible shape, you're getting the "stay away" signal, so take a step back literally and figuratively. Shoulders back, arms relaxed, knees slightly bent, or one foot forward gives you permission to take a baby step toward this more expansive stance. Approach with a willingness to step back if the vibration shifts.

Remind yourself to be careful about making a lot of physical contact in the very early stages. And smile (making sure your breath is particularly fresh so that it doesn't melt his contact lenses)!

When it comes to clothing, most of us have nutty stories about running into someone when we were over- or underdressed. Worrying about how you look at all times—"Just in case!"— is neurotic and narcissistic, which reminds me of one of my favorite wardrobe stories. I met this woman at a party, and we hit it off. When she mentioned that she wanted to find a gym to join, I invited her to be my guest one Saturday.

When we met that morning, I was in my usual workout gear: tights, a leotard, a T-shirt, shorts, and sneakers. Rather than commenting on the fact that she felt I was letting down womanhood as a whole with my horrifyingly casual getup, my new pal breathlessly and ponderously related the following tale: A friend of hers had been dating a gentleman for six months, during which she was always coiffed, perfumed, and elegantly dressed. However, one morning this poor woman went out to pick up her newspaper with her hair in curlers, and she ran into the guy—*"and he never called her again!"*

She told me this cautionary tale hoping that I'd be appropriately chastised and would change my wardrobe ways immediately—ceasing to wander around the city in exercise gear just because I was on my way to work out. I fear that I missed the point of her story: While I certainly wouldn't go to a party in my workout wear, if anyone I was dating found the sight of me in a leotard reason to dump me after six months, they're not the person for me. Bye-bye!

Dressing appropriately, cleanly, and neatly will do just fine when it comes to first impressions. A friendly smile, even if you aren't decked out in your very best finery, will also do quite nicely—especially if you're comfortable not only in your clothes, but in your own skin.

And now that we've covered these first impressions, let's get to the actual date itself.

CHAPTER 6
The First Date: Part I

Continuing on with our theme from the last chapter, let's keep assuming that you're just a glutton for punishment and really want your dating experience to be one of pain and suffering. Let's start with that all-important first date.

How?

If you really want to doom the date before you ever get it off the ground, the first thing to do is suggest that your intended might want to have sex with you immediately. Mentioning that it looks like it's been a long time since he's had a date never hurts either. Then there's always the obvious: "Haven't we met somewhere before?" or "I feel like I know you—I think we're soul mates." The old standbys "What's your sign?" and "Haven't I slept with you before?" are equally impressive.

"If I told you you had a beautiful body, would you hold it against me?" sounds good on a CD, so why not give it a try? Or going up to a cute guy and saying, "I was just playing a game of darts, and the loser had to buy you a drink," or "No one believed I had the nerve to ask you out," are both quite charming as well. Suggesting that everybody looks better closer to quitting time—or the lyrics of almost any country-and-western ditty—is a sure-fire people pleaser.

The good news is that if anyone actually took you up on any of these fabulous one-liners, you probably deserve each other—and if not, you've eliminated the possibility of suffering through a first date at all.

— Avoiding disasters: It's perfectly okay, legitimate, and even charming to admit that you're nervous. How you ask for the first date is really much less important than the fact that you are—repeat after me—*nonthreatening, friendly, and specific.* Saying, "Would you like to go out sometime?" is waste of stomach acid because you'll be nervous, and even if he says yes, you still have to ask him out for a specific time and place.

I can hear you saying, "Yeah, but if I'm specific and he says no, was it because of the time, or is he just not interested?" Good question . . . which you can actually pose to your seemingly reluctant conquest-to-be. In other words, to decrease some of the anxiety inherent in asking for a date, it's perfectly okay to be spontaneous and suggest getting a cup of coffee or an ice-cream cone, seeing a movie, or sharing a cab right now, this very minute: "Gee, this has been a really interesting art exhibit. If you're hungry, I'd love to buy you dinner."

Granted, spontaneity can increase refusals, so be prepared to be turned down due to scheduling, but you'll minimize the wear and tear on your nerves as well. You also have the option of offering an either/or: "If now isn't a convenient time, then maybe we could plan to do something next week?" And instead of asking, "Is it okay if I call you for a date?" try, "I'd love to take you to another gallery opening next week, or to the movie on Renoir that opens on Thursday." If you're going to go to the trouble of asking someone to reject you, you might as well give them something specific to respond to.

It never ceases to amaze me that men seem to feel that there's some magic combination of words that will guarantee dating success, when all women know that a well-rehearsed, slick line is much more likely to be a turnoff. Just saying, "I'm a little nervous about this, but I'd really like to spend some time with you," or "I'll never forgive myself if I don't ask you if you'd like to go get some ice cream," works really well. Admitting that you're uncomfortable or wish you had a cool line or were more poised makes you seem vulnerable, interested, and sincere—in other words, nearly irresistible.

If I haven't convinced you of the value of the simple and straightforward, I offer for your perusal the single best pickup line I've ever heard. I met a man at a party who confided, "I always compliment beautiful women on their brains and smart women on their beauty, and you're just so smart that I don't know where to start." He had me at "Hello!" He got triple credit: (1) He was revealing his line to me, making me his confidante by seemingly letting me see behind the scenes; (2) he gave me credit for being both beautiful and intelligent; and (3) he had the sense enough to realize that as an intelligent women, I was probably more comfortable about my intellect than my physicality. Brilliant line, but I basically feel now as I did then: I was in over my head. The world's cleverest pickup line didn't even work, so why bother? Instead, just go for simple and sincere. The odds are definitely in your favor.

Where?

There are two concerns to settle on immediately after you agree to date someone: location and activity. Let's start with the first one:

1. Location

Your place or mine? A noisy bar . . . or maybe a religious gathering? Anywhere that requires serious travel—including plane, train, or boat trips; pony express; covered wagons; bicycles; long car drives; and, my personal favorite, the Greyhound bus—are disaster incubators.

Here are some other absolutely terrible places to take people on a first date: a wedding (or better yet, *your ex's* wedding), a reunion, a company Christmas party (or any company function), a family gathering, a place where you have to give a speech, and believe it or not, to a movie or dinner. I know that you just did a double take, thinking, *Wow, a movie or dinner really doesn't really seem to fit into this category.* But, in fact, a movie is the world's worst place to go on a first date: You're going to spend most of your time sitting together in the dark, not even knowing if you're supposed to hold hands—then if you both like the movie, there's really nothing to talk about; and if you both hate the movie, there's really nothing to talk about either.

In addition, if neither of you has researched the movie, it's more than likely that one of you is going to find something offensive, overly sexual, or suggestive about it—thanks to the state of movies these days. Trust me, being a movie reviewer for the B.F.C.A. (Broadcast Film Critics Association), I've seen 'em all. You could ensure the absolutely foolproof disaster of the wrong movie for a first date by going to **www.drjoy.com** and clicking on movie reviews and either choosing one that's not listed (I only review ones I like) or picking one that's violent, appropriate for kids, or falls into any category that you think might offend either you or your date.

— Avoiding disasters: A movie is a great waste of a date, especially early on. Now, if it were up to me, everybody's first date would happen somewhere that both parties could comfortably talk (without getting shushed), walk around, and get to know each other with as little "required behavior" as possible. An art gallery, a fair, an amusement park, a botanical garden, a political campaign, or a dance lesson are all great first venues. I'm also a fan of "date-ettes," or short-term things that can be fairly spontaneous, so neither of you have much time to anticipate or get nervous.

Keep in mind that a first date doesn't have to be a planned marathon or the Bataan Death March. As long as the two of you are having a great time—and your date was relatively short, sweet, and easily accessible to begin with—it can be easily extended.

2. Activity

Since the all-American "date waste" is dinner and a movie, let's tackle the food situation. Eating in front of a person you barely know and want to impress is not the world's most comfortable experience. Every time your elbow bends, your mouth opens; and if you're paying, you're going to worry about whether the meal will exceed your budget. (Every female has been taught since the cradle to check out the right side of the menu first thing—and we all grew up eating chicken because it was the cheapest thing on that very side of the menu.) Everyone at the table feels pressured and on edge . . . and the food hasn't even arrived yet.

If you're absolutely determined that food has to be a part of the first date, then some particularly difficult restaurants to try are those that serve a lot of garlic, pasta, overly spicy dishes, or fried fare; any cuisine from a country that you can't readily identify on a map; any place that requires a bib, chopsticks, strolling mariachis, or special cooking implements; vegetarian restaurants; sports bars; and McDonald's or Chuck E. Cheese.

— **Avoiding disasters:** Okay, unless you're a complete idiot, you now know where you can go to eat because I've just told you all the places *not* to go! Look, because food is such a part of the American concept of dating, if you really want a nondisastrous venue, consider weekend brunch.

When?

The major poison here is duration. If you want to invite disaster (and I know you do), make a date interminable. These include marathons of any kind—dance; food; or the New York City, Boston, or Greek (the original 30 kilometers)—which will tip you both over the edge. Meeting the parents on the first date, as well as going out for the first time on Valentine's Day, New Year's Eve, or Christmas Eve, all have their potential for unrealistic expectations.

Saturday nights for a first date are like going from tennis for beginners directly to Centre Court at Wimbledon. Fridays are slightly less tense—at least we're only talking playoffs here. As Andrea, one of my radio callers, so eloquently shared, timing and the time spent can spell d-i-s-a-s-t-e-r:

> I met this guy at the grocery store and he seemed fine, so we decided to go out. He picks me up in his Corvette convertible—we start driving, and an hour goes by. Finally, I'm like, "Where are you taking me?" He was trying to take me to a seafood restaurant that's out in the middle of nowhere . . . and I don't even eat seafood.
>
> On the drive he seemed a little strange, a little aggressive. He couldn't find the restaurant, so he called and talked to a waitress to get directions, but since he couldn't really figure it out, he started to get really mad at her. Every time she'd give him a direction and he didn't know what she was talking about, he'd drive really, really fast and clench the steering wheel. I'm holding

on for dear life as he's screaming at the poor girl on the phone.

We finally get there, and I get the one chicken dish on the menu. When we leave, he tells me that he wants to stop by his house because he has something he wants to show me. He has me meet his parents! Then he reads me the "poems" he writes and tells me how he went on a vacation by himself—and I'm thinking, *Well, now I know why you went alone!*

— Avoiding disasters: Basically, what you want to do here is invite someone out for a first date on a Tuesday, Wednesday, or Thursday. Then, after you've been out a few times, getting together on a Friday or Saturday night points out that you aren't dating anyone else on those "serious date" nights. And daytime is less threatening (or sexy or serious) than nighttime when you're getting to know someone.

Saturday or Sunday brunch is a great idea, too: It fits the criteria of being in daylight, low-key, and of limited, but expandable, duration. (Okay, so brunch *is* food centered, but eggs or pancakes aren't all that messy to eat, are relatively inexpensive and readily available, and are quickly prepared.) Just keep in mind that the first date doesn't have to be on a Friday or Saturday night, and that evenings don't have to be the only time for a date. Pick a time that's easy, comfortable, and convenient for you both.

Finally, remember that people are busy. The fact that your date-to-be can't make the times you suggested shouldn't necessarily be a complete turnoff. If you've asked for two or three specific dates and he keeps saying no, and you have the sense that you aren't delusional—that is, he really does want to go out with you—you can say, "Hey, listen, I can't seem to be able to pick a good time for you. Would you be willing to pick a time and I'll accommodate you?"

What . . . (Am I Going to Wear)?

If you're really looking for the elements to doom-a-date, be sure that the event planned requires special clothing. Costume parties, formal events, pool parties, and so on are all recipes for early disaster.

— Avoiding disasters: Make sure that your clothing is clean, comfortable, and appropriate, and it doesn't send any message that you don't want it to. If you're the person making the date, be clear about what you're going to wear—it's okay to suggest the dress code so at least you'll match more or less. But be flexible; you can adjust. I've certainly gotten all dolled up, only to have my date show up in jeans. Yet since it was my house, I said, "Hey, you look casual . . . give me a minute," and then I changed clothes. (The person being collected can usually change clothes since their closet is the closest.)

If you happen to be meeting at the party or in a parking lot, and you turn out to be inappropriately or incompatibly dressed, forget about it! *Let it go.* Clothing is just to cover nakedness, and you can always make light of it by saying, "Listen, if you give me pointers next time, we can look like we came as a couple!"

I was recently at a reception at Carnegie Hall with a guy who had just gotten in from St. Bart's. He was very tan and wearing summer linens—on the coldest January day in 60 years. He apologized once, said he figured I looked so good that no one would notice him, and we both had a great time. (For more specifics about clothing after the first date, see page 96.)

Who?

This is the biggie, as whom you date is going to be set, if not in stone, at least definitively by how you behave the very first time you get together. It's so important, in fact, that it deserves its own chapter. Read on. . . .

CHAPTER 7
The First Date: Part II

When you actually get to that first date, there are so many possibilities for disaster that it can be hard to focus. Never fear: Dr. Joy is here with a chapter full of easy solutions.

Time

Being on time just shows that you're overeager, desperate, and have nothing else important going on in your life, so why would you want to have your date assume that about you? So be late! (Of course if you don't show up at all, that's called standing someone up, and that's really beyond doom—that's just tacky.) If you're the arriver, you want to be tardy enough to give the impression that you had better things to do, but because you're such a kind human being, you're going to keep a previously arranged commitment. After all, why not make 'em sweat?

In the old days, you could drive around the block 14 times or sit in someone else's driveway and just sort of let the moments tick by—but with cell phones, technology has made being late even classier and cooler. But don't even think about calling until at least a half hour *after* you're supposed to arrive. At that point, you may begin to call periodically to say that you're on your way, giving updates of your whereabouts, traffic, the weather, your gas gauge, whatever. If he seems to get testy, just tap the phone a few times and say, "Oh, you're breaking up. . . . I can't hear you, so I'll talk to you as soon as I can"—then show up when you're good and ready.

Naturally, you won't actually be showing up anytime soon. About every 15 minutes or so, call and point out that traffic hasn't cleared, your mother finally got off the phone, or you had to pick up your dry cleaning. It really doesn't matter what you say—and you don't even have to pretend to be sincere, since your date is going to know you probably aren't telling the truth. The important point is to just keep those excuses coming!

After about an hour, most people will have just left you in the lurch, so make sure that you call after, say, 55 minutes, and then pronounce, "Don't give up hope! I'm on my way!" Your date may be foolish enough to wait for you, so by the time you finally *do* arrive, look fairly glad to see him. A tinge of tension around the eyes demonstrates that whatever you were doing was really important, and clearly you've done him a huge favor by showing up at all. He'll be furious . . . and you'll be doomed.

A caller, Jolene, points out how miscommunication can make you feel as if this one's *never* gonna fly:

> I was in the service, and the guy I was going to go out with was as well, but he had a different schedule. We had to plan our

date a month and a half in advance. On my way to the date, my
car broke down and I couldn't get ahold of him. I tried and tried
but never got through. Three days later I ran into him and he was
like, "Well, I just figured you had something better to do."

Now, let's assume that for some unknown reason you can't pull off the
"I'm Joe Cool, I'm going to be late" performance. Or maybe you're really
curious about how your date-to-be handles stress. In either case, you can
be early! You want to see how somebody *really* looks when they're prepar-
ing to meet you, so arriving between a half hour and an hour ahead of time
will certainly get you what you're looking for. Again, cell phones can really
work here as well. Calling up a few hours prior to arrival time and saying,
"Hi! Just wanted to check to make sure we're still on . . . I'm right around
the corner!" will do nicely.

~~~ ~~~

If you're the arrivee, the same basic philosophy works, which is: Who
needs to be polite on a first date? Never, ever, be ready on time. Keeping
your date waiting, nearly endlessly, is a great idea. The longer you make him
cool his heels, the more he'll appreciate you when you finally do appear. If
he has any sense, he'll feel that you spent a huge amount of time prepar-
ing for him. Hey, you're worth it! (And if he's not outside waiting for you
with bated breath when you finally are ready . . . well, he probably wasn't
worth it anyway.)

On the other hand, if you just can't bring yourself to make the other person angry, then being ready extremely early is a great way to put *yourself* in a perfectly miserable mood. When your date arrives, even if he's on time, you'll be really pissed because you've been waiting for so long. Your makeup has started to dissolve, you're bored, you've bitten off all your nails . . . and you've had all the time in the world to convince yourself why you should have never made this date in the first place.

— **Avoiding disasters:** Just be on time—plus or minus no more than 15 minutes after the time you agreed on. And if you're going to be later than that, call *before* you were supposed to be there. Don't be a doofus— nobody likes to being kept waiting. If you wouldn't be late for a meeting with your boss, then don't be late for a date.

Attitude

Again, let's ignore any middle ground here. . . . Of course you're nervous and excited to see your date, but pull out all the stops and go for an Oscar here. Being larger than life, sexier than a Playmate, louder than Mt. Vesuvius, or more overbearing than Anna Nicole Smith is possible, but it does require a fair amount of energy. You might feel more at home as a shrinking violet, especially if cool isn't your first choice. If you're more of an insecure person, then go for it: After all, seeming to be needy *and* nerdy is really appealing. Since not everybody can be cool, some of us can be walking advertisements for antidepressants and social anxiety disorder.

If the eyes are the window to the soul, then make sure you don't look at your date—after all, you don't want him to see how uncomfortable you are. When you greet him, focus anywhere other than his eyes: His nose is a good choice; as is over his shoulder or yours, at the floor, at his shoes, or off into nowhere. This will allow you the protection you crave from prying eyes.

Also, make sure that your posture shows how completely nonthreatening you are: Stomach and butt both pooched out, knees slightly bent, toes curled inward, arms akimbo, shoulders hunched, and chin heading toward your chest will do the trick. And a limp handshake always works, especially if your palms are a bit sweaty or cold. Or you could try a bone crusher, especially in contrast to your lack of eye contact and nonthreatening posture. A little surprise will keep your date on his toes. If you're completely unsure about the handshake issue, just grab your date and give him a serious kiss . . . with tongue.

Finally, if you're really feeling insecure, it's always a good idea to show up with your dog, your best friend, or your mom. After all, first dates can be so taxing.

— Avoiding disasters: You know yourself better than anybody on this planet, so how you present yourself is going to be the single most important determinant on how somebody else sees you. If you enter a room like you're walking onto a yacht (as Carly Simon says), you're going to give a very different impression than if you're all hunched over, looking depressed, and being terrified that somebody will ask your name or your opinion. What this boils down to is that when you're meeting someone for the first time, make eye contact and extend your hand—even if your palms are a little sweaty, you're better off shaking a hand than not. And make sure that your posture is erect without being stiff.

When in doubt, check yourself out in front of a mirror, just like they do in the movies. You don't have to practice an opening line, since just saying "Hello" will always work. Don't feel that there's a perfect opening gambit, just make sure that you approach somebody the way that you'd like to be approached.

When I did a special for my book *Dating for Dummies* on the Discovery Channel, I actually had somebody practice approaching one of his roommates who was pretending to be a girl. Basically, what I had him do was try to keep his posture upright but relaxed. His chin was parallel with the floor, he made eye contact, and his arms were loosely swinging by his side. By doing the same, you'll look confident and relaxed as opposed to rigid, terrified, depressed, or any of the other negative possibilities.

Conversation

You've now gotten yourself to the door, so you're probably going to have to open your mouth and talk. Since all of us like to feel attractive and appreciated, flattering your date right away would get you in good with him right away . . . but since you're nervous and focused on yourself, it's easier to make sure that all compliments are generic and over the top.

If your date seems uncomfortable accepting your tributes, just heap more on. If you insist on being specific, then commenting on body parts (especially if you use generic, slang terms) allows you to be flattering, sexual, and humorous. (Being funny is a great way to go, especially when you have no idea of your date's sense of humor.) When in doubt, feel free to just say whatever comes to mind about your date's appearance: "Do you have keys in your pocket, or are you just happy to see me?" "Could that shirt *be* any tighter?" or "Guess you haven't been to the gym in a while" are great choices.

If your date has a zit or facial scars, certainly inquire into their origin. Asking about recent weight gain or loss, or if he always looks so tired or is perhaps just coming down with something are perfectly acceptable ways to begin. Other questions might be whether he's considered cosmetic dentistry or hair plugs—anything you can say to show that you're not one of those people who's intimidated by conventional manners.

Poignant observation is a way of making yourself stand out, branding yourself as a keen beholder of the human condition. Commenting on your date's home, funny-looking family pictures, pet, or cooking smells are nice ways to begin. And of course there's the ever-so-sleazy route of asking for a "tour" of his humble abode (in other words, "Can I see where you sleep?").

Life is short and unpredictable, which is why some of us order dessert first. So, if you want to be viewed as a real comer, don't waste time. In terms of opening gambits, one of the all-time classiest ways to go is asking right off the bat if your date is going to have sex with you. Why not cut to the chase?

— **Avoiding disasters:** Most people are thrilled to be complimented, but understand that if you're going to do so you must be specific, sincere, and not focused on any particular body part. Complimenting men on their haircut, their eyes, or even their socks and shoes are all acceptable. (Although I must say I did have a date with a man once who never forgave me for saying that I knew he wasn't gay because his shoes were too ugly!)

Commenting on your surroundings, the weather, other people at a party (making sure that you're not being mean), a painting, a wall color, the food, or the band that's playing can make great conversation starters, but using wit on an early date is always a bit problematic. Even for those of us with a good sense of humor, we have no idea what someone we hardly know will find funny. You're better off getting to know each other slowly and gently before you attempt to kid anybody about anything. Even self-deprecating humor can be interpreted as insecurity. If you're absolutely determined to tell a joke, make sure it has nothing to do with ethnicity, politics, race, or sex. (For a more in-depth look at the uses and abuses of humor, see the next chapter.)

A question is a good conversational tool as long as it isn't too personal and can't be answered by a simple yes or no, leaving you right back where you started. In other words, "What's your favorite movie that you've seen lately?" is a much better question than "Have you seen any good movies lately?" And if you're going to ask questions, make sure that you listen to what he says, as opposed to doing what a famous broadcaster does: You can hear her mentally checklisting her questions because she views her queries as far more interesting than anyone else's answers.

Letting someone actually finish a sentence without interruption is both polite and a good idea, and also demonstrate that you're interested in what he has to say and have no particular need to control the conversation. Allowing the discussion to find its own level enables you both to be relaxed and enjoy being together without having to fill every moment with talk. Also, keep in mind that when women are nervous, we tend to speak faster, while men tend to clam up. So be a little patient when asking someone a question—then give him time to come up with an answer.

Chemistry
(and We Aren't Talking about Sexual Attraction)

It's perfectly normal to be a bit nervous about this dating thing. Even if you're trying to be cool, everybody knows that dating is really a high-risk endeavor. Now why should you have to worry your pretty little head about this when there are modern miracles (as well as old-fashioned remedies) available to you as near as your medicine cabinet, liquor store, or neighborhood dealer? That's right: Be drunk or high on your date. Certainly the classic way of calming one's nerves in our country is better living through chemistry—

so if you're a little nervous, stopping at the neighborhood bar for a couple shots, taking your favorite downer, or having a quick hit of some illegal substance are all certainly ways of calming down. In other words, if cool is hard for you to come by naturally, come by it artificially!

If one drink gives you enough courage to get there, then two will make you fearless. And the fact that people can smell it on you should in no way deter you—a couple of breath mints will completely fool your date into thinking that you're stone-cold sober. And if you're waiting for someone, hey, hitting the cooking sherry to get rid of those pre-date jitters is a great thing to try. Your date will probably never figure it out . . . and if he does, well, just think of how relaxed *you'll* be.

— **Avoiding Disasters:** Let Natalie, a caller on my show, show you the way on this one:

> My roommate fixed me up with this guy. During dinner we had some wine, and then we had some more. Then we went to a cocktail bar, and I ended up drinking myself silly. It was terrible—and really, really embarrassing. So he managed to get me back to my apartment, but before we got in, I vomited in the elevator . . . and he cleaned it up!
>
> He finally got me upstairs; my roommate was shocked of course. So I stumbled in and yelled, "I have to get my pajamas on," and proceeded to undress in front of him. He turned around like a perfect gentleman, said good-bye to my roommate, and left.

The next day, I called when I knew he wasn't going to be home and left a message that said, "I am so sorry. I'm mortified. It was really nice meeting you."

Alcohol is the great solvent of the superego (that part of you that knows not to do what you're about to do), as well as a depressant of the central nervous system. If your date has only seen you when you've been drunk or high, not only is he going to have no idea who you are, but you're not going to have any idea who he is or how the two of you interact with one another. In our society, stone-cold sober isn't billed as being that much fun, but if you're trying to make some decisions about things like a second date, for example, being sober may make a huge amount of sense. (Not to mention the problem of driving drunk or high—I mean, it really makes no sense to wrap either of you around a telephone pole.)

These days, we're ridiculously committed to romance. One of my favorites examples is in this TV ad: A gorgeous woman in a glamorous, flowing gown is sitting in front of a beautiful table set with linen, crystal, and a single perfect rose, as filmy curtains waft in the background. This handsome fellow in a tux makes smoldering eye contact with her from across the room. As he saunters in, eyes locked on hers, he accidentally pulls the tablecloth off the table. The wine does a half gainer, spilling all over the floor. It turns out that this commercial is really for a stain remover! But it says so much about our notion of romance and love by poking fun at the soft-focus, slightly blurred, lack-of-hard-edges picture that makes us believe this is a love story.

Soft focus isn't a way to date. Sooner or later—and sooner is much better than later—you'll want to know the real you, *both* of you, and you'll want your date to know the reality as well. Dating is indeed a high-risk behavior, so you'll want and need every faculty you have about you to bring to the party. Leave the drugs in the '70s, and save the champagne toast for New Year's Eve.

Personal Hygiene

There's so much potential for disaster here that I've broken this section down into three parts. Let's look at the body first.

1. The Body

When human beings get nervous, our hearts beat fast, our mouths get dry, our tummies flutter, and we sweat. In the animal kingdom, this is known as the fight-or-flight response, in which rapidly metabolizing muscles generate excess heat—but in the dating kingdom, it's just nature's way of saying "I'm really glad to see you." But if you want to be Joe Cool, know that antiperspirants, deodorants, and even showers are for suckers. Going natural is a great test to see if your date can appreciate the *real* you.

Okay, so you figure that after three hours of chasing your kid brother around the yard on a hot summer day, that may be asking a bit much of even your nostrils, yet you're running a bit late. What should you do? Well, as Europeans figured out centuries ago (before the advent of modern plumbing), a little scent dabbed here and there could win over the faint of heart—the fact that it's called "toilet water" should in no way deter you. *Toilette* means more "grooming" than "commode" in French, so pour it on. Just come prepared so that when he has an allergy attack, you can look like a real class act by offering him some tissues.

As one of my callers, Jonathon, succinctly described, birds of a feather don't necessarily soar on the same clouds of perfume together:

> I met a very nice girl at a party and asked her out for the following Saturday. I found her apartment, rang the bell, and discovered that they had a canary flying around the apartment. I have sort of a fear of birds, so I couldn't get out of there fast enough! We left and went to the movies. It was a hot summer night and the theater had no air conditioning, which wouldn't have been that bad—except that my date had doused herself with Dollar-a-Gallon perfume. This stuff started to hit me right in the gut. I made it through the movie, but my insides were churning, and it was getting worse and worse. I was about to barf when she asked me back to her place for coffee, which meant that I was going to have to face that bird again.
>
> We got closer to her house, and I was trying to figure out how to basically dump this girl without being cruel. So we were going up one of these steep hills when it occurred to me. I

started slowing down, and then I put my foot on the clutch so that the car started to roll back. I shrieked, "Oh my God, these hills have burned out my clutch!" I let the car roll backward into a parking space and said, "It looks like we're going to have to call it a night—I have to get this car towed."

I walked her partway to her apartment, ran back to the car, and drove home . . . and that night has never left me. To this day, when I smell that perfume, I feel sick.

If you've been reading in current medical journals that tension can create stomach problems causing bad breath—know that breath mints are for wimps. Also, the notion that what you had for lunch or dinner may remain on your breath shouldn't bother someone like you. Garlic, smoke, coffee, chocolate, alcohol, and onions all give a clue to the real you . . . and possible dinner selections! There's no particular reason to cover them up.

Understand that a little anxiety just makes you more attractive, and if your breath goes sour—hey, you aren't planning to kiss anyone anytime soon, right? Scraping your tongue is gross because bacteria gotta live, too, and as for the old choppers, when in doubt, go casual: Broccoli in your front teeth shows that you eat your veggies, so why brush or floss? The point is that teeth are for chewing food, and if any particles remain, then it just proves that you're human.

Finally, unwanted hair, dirty fingernails, and a female five o'clock shadow (on legs, armpits, or anywhere else you can grow it) bespeak a casual disregard for conventional mores and uptight parental rules.

— **Avoiding disasters:** Understand that if cleanliness isn't next to godliness, it's certainly next to a respectable comfort level—as well as indicating an adult character. When in doubt, make sure that you smell lovely. This doesn't mean putting a whole lot of scent on; it means making sure that you've bathed recently; have used deodorant (and you may want to invest in an antiperspirant, too); and have brushed your teeth, flossed, and used mouthwash. Your teeth should also have been professionally cleaned within the last millennium.

The idea here is that the first impression you give is not only visual, but it's olfactory as well. I had a professor in medical school who, whenever he saw a patient, would get up and walk around the desk and shake hands with him or her. He did this so that he could feel the texture of their skin, could see whether or not their eyes were jaundiced, and could smell their breath. Bad breath can come from any number of different origins, but you can tell a lot about a person by what their breath smells like. And you don't want people to know anything about you except that you're clean!

If you have a problem with breath, as many people do, look first to your diet, since there are definitely foods and spices that can affect it (including garlic, onions, tobacco, chocolate, and coffee). If it's a persistent problem, it could also have to do with nerves, so an antacid may help you out. However, seeing your dentist and doctor isn't a bad idea, because there are a number of medical situations that can cause bad breath that really need to be treated—and you certainly don't want to be worrying about this on a date.

Asking your best friend to give you a once-over or to check your breath before a date is certainly the mark of a true pal. He or she could also make sure you didn't overdo it with the scent, which so many people are actually allergic to these days. After all, the more confident you are beforehand, the more comfortable you'll be on the date.

2. Clothing

We briefly covered clothing selection in an earlier section, but here I'd like to focus on a more nuts-and-bolts, "sniff test" approach. Now that we've covered your nakedness . . . let's *cover* your nakedness.

If clothes make the woman, why look desperate by wearing starched and pristine apparel? I mean, you'll just give your date the impression that you really care. Show him the real you: If you've been doing some gardening, been out jogging, or have spilled something on your shirt, show up as is. Let him see that you're a woman of the people. Being a little worn around the edges adds distinction, so arrive less than sartorially splendored. Scuffed shoes, stockings with runs, drooping hems, unraveling cuffs, sweat-stained tops, and dirty tennies go with anything, anytime, especially if you plan on loading up on the bling, too.

What you wear on a date will determine not only how comfortable you are but also how at ease your date is. If you're the one who arranged the evening, you know what the dress code is going to be at the particular place you're thinking about going, but when in doubt (and telling your date just lessens the surprise), simply dress down. If most people are going to be dressed in elegant evening wear, why bother? Broadcast how really cool you are by showing up in jeans, tennis shoes with the laces undone, your favorite T-shirt (which has those lovely "ventilation holes" under the arms), and a baseball cap. Don't worry—these days, unisex is where it's at.

Conversely, you can go all out and strut your stuff. A ball gown, a tiara, and a feather boa are always a good idea, even if it's for a summer barbecue. (After all, I have an aunt who's always felt that the best way to get a guy to take you to a nice restaurant is to dress up.) And if the two of you are completely mismatched, it's just a way of finding out how you deal with compromise!

Carrie, one of my callers, points out sartorial (and chemical) pitfalls:

> I was 18 years old working as a cashier on Valentine's Day. A gentleman came into the store and asked me out. I thought, *What the heck—it's Valentine's Day, and I don't have a date.* He picked me up, and he's wearing these white tight pants and a blue blazer, but I told myself that I was going to get over the clothing and not let it bother me. We go to the local bar and have a couple of drinks, and I was starting to get a little tipsy and giggly. But the date is really going nowhere, so I wanted to go home. We left, but I had to go to the bathroom really badly. Conveniently, the guy lived a block away from the bar, so we went upstairs, and I went to the bathroom. When I came out,

he was at his piano with just the blazer and pants on—no shirt—singing Billy Joel's "She's Always a Woman to Me." Then he proceeded to try to kiss me. As he wrestled me to the ground, I hit my head on the coffee table.

Now to the biggie: How tight should your clothing be? Well, when in doubt, let spandex be your guide! And know that visible panty lines (VPL) are also always attractive. Underwear that can be plainly seen because the outer covering is too tight, too sheer, too light, or too low will instantly brand you as a fashion hottie. If you choose to wear insanely provocative clothing, hey, at least the two of you will have something to talk about!

— **Avoiding disaster:** Beware of deciding that you're going to "wow" your escort with your clothes. Wearing a lot of jewelry on a first date is also not a great idea. I actually had a date tell me that he once dated a woman who wore a lot of jewelry on their first date, and when he commented on it she said, "Yes, an old boyfriend gave it to me—but if you'd like to replace it, I'd love to wear *your* jewelry." I think that defines tacky.

3. Environs

A date is, by nature, unpredictable. It's important to be prepared (or unprepared, as the case may be) for any eventuality. For example, a date may begin or end on your turf, and while making someone wait outside does add a certain cachet, you may as well be prepared to let 'em see that you're neither prissy nor uptight, but live life to the fullest. You're a free thinker, so make sure that your house hasn't been artificially straightened just for him—and don't let your devil-may-care attitude stop there.

The following touches show the real you: a lawn that hasn't been cut, trash that hasn't been taken out (or that's in bags that have been ripped apart), pet hair or droppings, last year's Christmas decorations and, of course, the ever-popular car up on blocks or a broken pink flamingo out front. Make sure the doorbell is broken—in a pinch, a smashed window will work as well.

Once he comes inside your house or apartment, be sure that the front room has that "comfortably lived in" look. Dust bunnies bespeak nonchalance, as well as a love of *all* living things. Ex-boyfriends' underwear, and used food containers, tastefully strewn about can be the path to a bedroom where the sheets are suitably rumpled and seasoned, while the room itself is carpeted with your worn and discarded—but not forgotten!—clothes.

Since dating is a high-wire act that causes appropriate body responses, your date may need to use the bathroom, and sending him to the local gas station may be considered a bit hostile. So make sure that there are those little toothpaste mints all over the inside of the sink, and dead and discolored soap bubbles that illustrate your free spirit. A toothbrush whose bristles have long since died, scum around the bathtub, tile that needs desperately to be regrouted, and that empty toilet-paper roll make a strong statement, along with grimy towels that emanate that lovely mildew smell. Nice touch.

(**Author's note:** *I once had a guy ask to take a shower at my house. I guess he thought that the idea of his getting naked in my house would turn me on. Wrong! Nevertheless, the bathroom still needs to be tidy.*)

～～ ～～

Finally, if dating is a peculiar American phenomenon (which it certainly is), then dating in a car is part of the American landscape. Only wimps check out their vehicle to make sure that the tires are inflated, that there's actually gas in the little sucker, that you can't see the pavement through the floorboards, and that your beloved conveyance doesn't have to be jump-started by putting it in neutral and pushing it down the hill. Making sure that your car is date-ready just makes you look overeager, so don't worry about any of those pesky mechanical things. And, if nothing else, your ride breaking down just gives you more insight into how your date acts in a crisis.

Beyond the mechanical, you can also instantly find out how much he's focused on the cosmetic parts of life. So make sure that your car hasn't been washed recently. Of course, you can take care of any smell with that little pine-tree air freshener. As long as all the junk is in the backseat, he'll never notice. Just tuck those empty beer cans, half-eaten Big Macs, and junk-food wrappers under the seat.

— **Avoiding disasters:** Just make sure that your environs are neat and tidy! You certainly don't have to wallpaper the bathroom just because you have a date, but you may want to clean the scum out of the bathtub. I know that a shower curtain can cover a multitude of sins, but keep in mind that there are an awful lot of people who are curious enough to peek behind the curtain.

Also, while being seen as hospitable is always a good idea, it's not wise to spend a whole lot of time at either of your homes when you're first getting to know each other. It sends unclear signals, as everyone knows that there's a bedroom around someplace. While bedrooms may be an eventual destination on a date, early on is not a great idea.

Money

In theory, money is simply that dirty, green paper stuff that just lies there, except it isn't—it's power, lifestyle, choice, tradition, style, structure, independence (or dependence), and a whole lot more. But don't be intimidated! I can show you three ways to build a disaster from the get-go—with or without an ATM card.

1. **Arrive penniless,** muttering that you didn't have time to hit the cash machine. Or you could make sure that you don't mention you have no money until it actually comes time to buy the theater tickets or the gas or pay for dinner. If you're a really good actor, you can go through the whole Meryl Streep routine and say, "Oh my God! I thought I had some cash with me!" Or you could just play it cool and say, "You know what? Forgot to hit the ATM. How about you get this one? I'll get the next one." Yeah, right!

2. **Be chintzy.** You can easily doom your date by offering to split the check—especially if you're the one who ordered drinks, wine, appetizers and dessert, while your date only had a salad. And splitting the check means splitting it down the middle, not having separate checks, where you each pay for your own meal. (On the other hand, you can suggest separate checks if you ordered less than your date.)

Show your true colors: If you're the type who's very careful with money, find an inexpensive restaurant and make sure that you have a half-price coupon—and then offer to split the check. You can also pattern yourself after the guy who invited a woman I know for dinner, picked her up, told her he'd already eaten, wasn't very hungry and was on a low-carb diet anyway, so could they just have a drink? At the restaurant, she suggested an appetizer; he declined and went to the bathroom. She was so miffed that she ordered everything on the menu and ate it. When the time came for the check, she excused herself to powder her nose and disappeared.

3. **Be totally extravagant.** Pick something wildly expensive that you'll never be able to afford again. I had a friend who, on a first date, took the woman to the Metropolitan Opera (tickets were about 150 bucks apiece) and dinner ($300) in a rented a limousine ($300). The question was, what was he going to do for a second date? Buy her a small country?

— **Avoiding disasters:** The issue of money is certainly a major one, not only in dating but in relationships and society in general. Everybody thinks that the cause of the breakup of most first marriages is sex, but it's actually money. As I mentioned earlier, it represents lifestyle, choice, power, upbringing, convention, tradition, dependence, dominance, control, security, leisure, and gobs more. It's all sorts of things that have nothing to do with the fact that it's green, inert, and just lies there.

My basic rule of thumb for dating and money is that he who asks pays. Do what you can afford, which allows for comfort and staying well within your budget. There's certainly nothing attractive about people being chintzy, and we've already talked about how tacky it is to split checks. It's perfectly okay to offer to contribute when the check comes, or to say, "If you'd like me to get this one, you could get the next one," or to offer to take care of the tip. It's also perfectly all right to allow your date to pay. But just because he makes more money doesn't mean that he should pay all the time.

Finally, showing your interest in this person by putting in time, effort, thought, and resources into making sure that he has a good time is a really important part of dating. How much you actually spend shouldn't be relevant to either of you.

~~~~ ~~~~

Okay, now you know exactly how to doom any date, but why be confined to specific scenarios? Let's widen the perspective and take on the entire,

big, fat, sloppy world in order to positively ensure that you have the philo-
sophical underpinnings and wherewithal to feel confident in your ability to
really mess up anything date-wise.

So I bring you the Next Toxic Step. Ta-dah!

CHAPTER 8

The Next Toxic Step:
Nine Power Tools

I've taken you through the personals and the decalogue of dunces, and I've gone to the mountaintop and returned with how to doom a date from the very beginning. What now? Well, how about a toxic toolbox right there by your side, strapped to your waist and guarding your privates, which will allow you the minimal amount of thought or effort to dig down and doom yourself—not only on dates, but in *any* social situation whatsoever that may come your way. In other words, it's toxic dating and beyond!

The power tools of dating are actually all power *abuses:* bullying, anger, arguments, tantrums, sarcasm, arrogance, criticism, jealousy, and pretense. Of course, all eight of these tools just serve to cover up your insecurities, but your adversary—whoops, I mean *date*—doesn't have to know that. You're never gonna let him see you sweat.

Getting Started

There are those who will tell you that moving from friendship to romance is the best way to date, since it allows you to lay the groundwork for trust by getting to know someone slowly and carefully. Friendship is one of the few human relationships based on an equality of power and, unlike acquaintanceship, is designed for longevity, resilience, and hardiness—thus, it's more straightforward and organic, proceeding easily and surely from one step to another while taking the necessary time, care, and patience. Being friends first is supposed to be a stable, reasonable basis from which to catapult into romance because it requires a small leap from knowledge to intimacy, rather than the other way around. Pay no attention to the fools who tell you such nonsense—they have no idea what they're talking about!

If you're one of those people who's dating mostly to notch your own belt or to justify your mother's feeling that no one will ever love you—or your own sense that the opposite sex is no damn good—then this is the chapter for you! Here we're going to discuss what to do in any situation across the board to play kamikaze, scorched-earth, take-no-prisoners, slash-and-burn dating, regardless of which of the previously discussed charmers you've found to go out with.

These are the tried-and-true rules that are absolutely guaranteed to sabotage any relationship from the very beginning so that you avoid intimacy, wrestle control, and make damned sure that you're not the vulnerable one.

In nature, an animal shows weakness by baring its neck, the most vulnerable part of the body, because if the jugular vein is attacked, exsanguination (bleeding to death) is quick, nasty, and certain. By being close enough to be attacked and baring that part of its body, it signals its willingness and intention to be close and nonthreatening, giving up any pretense of security or aggression. Since you obviously don't want that to happen to you, these eight tools will offer outstanding protection.

1. Bullying

Being a bully becomes attractive once you feel that you're not going to be able to get what you want by reason, logic, or good behavior. Granted, healthy relationships balance vulnerability, intimacy, and power . . . but who needs a healthy relationship?! Convincing someone that you have them under your thumb when you're feeling vulnerable shifts the balance in your favor. And never forget that using power to get what you want has an old and storied history: Just whip out your plastic, your superiority (intellectual, moral, or cultural), your willingness to walk out, or anything else that will scare the daylights out of your date, and you're assured success.

— **Avoiding disasters:** If you know what you want, can be specific, and respect yourself *and* your partner, then negotiation and compromise can be exciting, exhilarating, challenging, and fun. The need to dominate and control (which is basically a pretty lonely position) will then be replaced by the sense that you won't be harmed or abandoned.

2. Anger

Anger is perfectly fine, but here we're talking about the use and abuse of a technique for controlling a situation by making someone feel endangered emotionally. It's pretty direct: Just holler and scream and bulge that cute little vein in your forehead. If somebody asks you a question, you can either ignore their impudence or bellow, "I don't have to answer that!" Eye contact can be simplified to staring or the ever-popular glaring. On the other hand, if this seems to take too much energy, there's a second option (and my personal favorite). This more manipulative form of anger is best exemplified by the mother who says, "Don't worry about me . . . you do what you want—I'll be okay." What she's really saying is, "If you don't do what I want, you'll never get a date, be happy, or make *me* happy ever again as long as you live. I'm your mother! I went through very painful labor to have you, so you owe me. And don't you ever forget it."

The advantage of passive-aggressive anger is that you don't have to do very much, which forces your date to do all the work. No matter what he does or says, all you have to do is sigh, "Fine" or "Whatever," sounding world-weary, disappointed, and blasé—but too well brought up to point out his shortcomings. What you basically do (and this is the beauty of the passive-aggressive "thang") is nothing. No energy needs to be expended.

As for anyone who has the audacity to persist in questioning or otherwise trying to engage you, simply counterattack by demanding, "What do you mean by that?" And the appropriate eye contact for the passive-aggressive is quite simple: Don't make any!

— **Avoiding disasters:** Be aware that in our society, men tend to accept their rage, while women tend to accept their sadness—if you can understand the link between the two, then you may be able to dig a little deeper and figure out that part of anger or aggression is really sadness. (Passive-aggressiveness, which masquerades as sadness, especially falls into this category.)

Understanding the distinction between anger and sadness is crucial because if you're demonstrating anger, your date will feel the need to fight with you—but if you're really feeling sad, this will only serve to make you feel even more vulnerable. However, if you're expressing sadness, then his tendency will be to try to comfort you—and if you are indeed angry, that's going to feel very claustrophobic. You can see why it's important—not only in terms of a relationship, but in terms of communication and knowing yourself as well—to understand the distinction.

Of course, no one's happy all the time, just like nobody's always sad. Being unfailingly perky can be a way of keeping others at arm's length—along with your own emotions. Lavish compliments to strangers, friends, and waiters symbolize insecurity. We humans aren't perfect creatures—we all have strengths and weaknesses, as well as things that make us happy and unhappy. This is part of the pleasure of discovery in a relationship. If you're so dedicated to keeping people at bay, either by your aggression or by your niceness, you're never going to know anyone.

3. Arguments

Arguing is a way of exerting your intelligence, power, and importance. The subject matter is usually irrelevant—a loud disagreement always asks the unspoken question, "What about me?" Debating your partner's feelings by telling him how he feels is key to determining who's in charge of the relationship. If he floats out a statement that seems meaningless to you, argue with it. And keep practicing—nothing is too trivial to fight about. After all, quarreling is one of those skills that everyone should keep sharp. The fact that you're always at each other's throats just adds excitement and variation to the relationship.

Also, keep making your partner defend himself. If you want to, in the middle of an argument you can change your position completely and see if you can't confuse him. If nothing else, it shows your ability to change your opinion on a dime. (Lawyers are particularly good at this.)

— **Avoiding disasters:** I was a debater in high school and actually won trophies for it. When I started dating, I thought, *Well, this is great. I know* *men aren't always comfortable dealing on an emotional level, and since I feel equally at home with logic or emotion, I'll give them home-field advantage by dealing with them in a logical way.* So a guy I dated would say something logical, and I'd giggle and think, *This is going to be fun! I'll just take the opposite point of view so that we can examine both sides.* I'd do so, and the guy would repeat his logical statement more forcefully. And I'd think, *Wow, he's ready to play!* So we'd be off and running, with me having a ball and being incredibly proud of myself for being so versatile . . . while he got louder and more red in the face.

What I didn't understand—and what took me much too long to figure out—was that for some people, arguing is a way of asserting dominance. So when I differed with the guys I dated, for them it was about winning— and while I thought of it as playful, they didn't. If I was somehow more adept than they, I'd find them going for my jugular, or they'd just get sullen and walk away.

Arguments are a waste of energy. Instead, there are ways of discussing (and disagreeing) that don't carry such emotional weight. For example, if you and your date have a difficult time agreeing on something, try changing points of view and see where you get. Put yourself in his shoes just for a moment, because it's helpful to see where he's coming from. Remember that most people are much more likely to listen to another point of view, provided that it's presented calmly, quietly, and specifically.

4. Tantrums

When I started to write this book, my first inclination was to put temper tantrums in the Mama's Boy section, then I decided to go with the Dance-Away Lovers (specifically the Manic-Depressive and the Addict). I finally decided that tantrums are ubiquitous enough to warrant their own section.

The advantage of throwing a fit is that you can orchestrate a *Titanic*-sized sinking ship of disaster. Thinking of yourself as an out-of-control two-year-old allows you to guarantee that if you're not getting what you want, neither will anyone else. Toddlers are making a major lurch toward independence by separating for the first time from Mom, thereby discovering the difference between themselves and others. Of course children still crave, and depend on, Mom's attention, closeness, love, and praise—but they also yearn to be able to explore the world on their own.

Two-year-olds can't negotiate for what they want because not only is Mom big and smart, but the children don't have the words to express, let alone achieve, what they want. So what do any self-respecting toddlers do? Throw oatmeal on the floor, scream, say no, cry, or hold their breath, all of which work beautifully. The youngsters have singlehandedly stopped the flow, distracted Mom (especially if it's the first time), and elicited a hug or a call to Dad. Whoo-hoo! Victory *and* hugs . . . and since it worked once, why not try it again?

Little kids instinctively understand that they have no power except to sulk, sabotage, and scream, and in so doing, they're able to bring everything and anything to a screeching halt. The more public the place, the more effective the strategy—in other words, the grocery store, church, the bus stop, and Grandma's house are all settings that work just beautifully. A toddler throwing a fit in a public place immobilizes everyone, so very little can be accomplished. Attempting to calm the child just reinforces the tantrum by essentially admitting: "Well, you wanted attention, and now you've got it." Hollering to combat it simply becomes the battle of the babies, and any sane adult knows that the only solution is a pasted-on smile, gritted teeth, and a quick but fervent prayer for the earth to open up immediately. Okay, so in the long run, not much is accomplished, but two-year-olds aren't known for taking the long view. Realistically, all a parent can do is ignore the kid and walk a short distance away, pretending that he or she is someone else's. *Nobody* will attempt to kidnap a child in full tantrum mode.

By the same token, if you feel that you have no power in your relationship, why not try guerilla tactics? If you see yourself as weak, then throwing a temper tantrum will reinforce this. And yeah, the same general rules apply to the grown-up version of a two-year-old as well. Placating is reinforcing, and you might get sex or attention or hugs temporarily. You may be able to incite a screaming match that allows you to both become large, green, scary Incredible Hulks, feeding off each other's impotence, frustration, and anger—as well as your ability to reduce each other to out-of-control, uncivilized two-year-olds.

— **Avoiding disasters:** Given the fact that everyone really does want their own way—and we know that creating a scene or trying to embarrass or demean someone else is not a way of getting it—how should you get yours? The answer is to be very specific about what you want. Instead of demanding, "Listen to me!" you can say, "It's really important to me that we talk about which restaurant we go to tonight." It's a very different kind of statement. Once you're talking about going for Chinese or French food, then you can decide to do Chinese tonight and French tomorrow, compromise on Mexican, or order in; or you can both decide to go your separate ways and meet for a movie.

Rather than deciding that you have to have your own way, all you really need to do is understand what it is that you want and be willing to decide what's negotiable and what's not. Then you have a basis for not only a relationship, but for evaluating the future of that relationship. If everything has to be negotiated, you've got a problem. However, if the two of you can agree to disagree on certain things but there's a great deal of commonality, then you don't have to worry about power and negotiations.

There's a great story about Henry Kissinger and President Nixon, who had an Irish setter named King Timahoe. (Having loved dogs my whole life, and having had several Irish setters, I can tell you that they're lovely creatures, but they ain't the sharpest knife in the drawer.) Apparently, King Timahoe came into the Oval Office while Kissinger was talking to Nixon and started scratching the carpet. Nixon said, "Cut it out," and the dog kept scratching. With more force, Nixon ordered, "Stop it!" The dog kept scratching, and Nixon shouted, *"Stop it right now!"* Then he opened his desk drawer and threw the dog a bone, which made him stop scratching.

Kissinger reportedly said, "Congratulations—you've just taught the dog to scratch three times and you'll toss him a bone."

In the face of a tantrum, all one can really do is walk away. It's the only sensible response to such behavior. Anything else means that you've taught the little monster what will work next time. With a temper tantrum, any kind of attention is reinforcing because all God's children would rather be praised than punished, but they'd rather be punished than ignored. So it's best to ignore someone who's causing a scene, and head them off at the pass by reinforcing positive behavior. (If you're with someone who believes that physical strength can or should be used to attain what he wants in a relationship, then get out, get safe, and get right with your head.)

5. Sarcasm

To be sarcastic, you've got to be a bit older—as well as more verbal, sophisticated, and smart—than a two-year-old . . . but what's toxic behavior without a bit of a challenge?

Nasty humor is universal, and another lovely way to get what you want without much heavy lifting—in other words, it's another way of acting out that allows you to exert control even when (or maybe *especially* when) you're feeling powerless. Make sure that your jokes are mean, pointed, and embarrassing—anything that you find even faintly funny should be shared openly, loudly, and initially. Sarcasm in foreign languages is always okay, as it not only shows your sense of humor, but how much smarter you are than everybody else. Ethnic jokes are also a surefire hit, as well as those having to do with your date's age and sex.

If one joke doesn't work, try another—and don't in any way be deterred by your date's raising his eyebrows or looking appalled. That's just his way of showing appreciation. If you want to make sure that you're getting your point across, elbowing him, slapping him on the back, or laughing in his face is a great way of cementing the fact that you have an excellent sense of humor.

— **Avoiding disasters:** Sarcasm is a way of gaining power in a situation because it means that you're imposing your worldview on your date. Then he really only has two choices: He can either laugh, at which point he's agreed with you; or he can be offended, at which point you can say that he has no sense of humor. Heads you win, tails he loses.

Instead of using sarcasm, get to know who this person is and if there are things that you both can find funny. And when in doubt, turn the humor on you: Making a joke about yourself may be self-demeaning, but it's going to be a lot funnier than poking fun at someone else.

Sarcasm is humor's ugly cousin, and it has no place in loving relationships—period.

6. Arrogance

All God's children are insecure. Please reread, memorize, and use this sentence to your benefit. Hide your own insecurities behind bravado, posturing, and most important, by remembering and acting out on the fact that the best defense is a good offense. In other words, be arrogant whenever possible: at the first twinge of your own insecurities; at even the most minor hint of anyone else's; and, crucially, at the first whisper of mutiny against your all-knowing and all-beingness. Since women worry about how they look and men worry about losing face, arm yourself accordingly.

You can best deal with your insecurities by deciding that anybody who's with you is your soul mate, reflecting you exactly—and if they truly love you, then they won't only be your biggest fan, head cheerleader, and major worshiper, but they'll also love *all* your choices and mirror your taste precisely. Assert how special you are by pointing out that you've moved beyond traditional role models, which allows you to question your date's behavior—and his job is to realize that, while also constantly offering you the affirmation you need and deserve.

Never allow anyone around you to giggle—it's not respectful. And since you deserve respect, envy, and whatever you want whenever you want it, it's well worth the effort to pick huge fights if your date should question any of your choices and preferences, no matter how seemingly trivial. These include, but aren't limited to, your favorite spice (go for cumin—it sounds nasty), movie, rock band, haircut, or color; or the morality of anyone who prefers oldies over talk radio. Disapprove loudly and often, and don't allow even a minor divergence from your party line.

Being tough about meaningless choices will camouflage your insecurities in other areas, as well as keeping everything off balance. The best way to keep your date from discovering the real you (the quivering, insecure mess) is to keep him constantly on his toes—so be inconsistent, critical, and emotionally over-the-top at all times. Attack, attack, attack.

— **Avoiding disasters:** While it's true that all of us *are* insecure, we each show it in a different way. So if you're really trying to work through a relationship and make it positive rather than negative, first be aware of your own insecurities—because if you aren't, you're very likely to project them onto another person. For example, if you feel that your mouthwash has failed, if the other person takes a step back, you're going to take it personally. But with an awareness of your own perceived soft spots, you can just say something like, "Gee, did my mouthwash fail?" rather than beating a hasty retreat or deciding that your date hates you. Self-awareness allows for *communication*.

That doesn't mean that it's cool to broadcast all your insecurities to anyone who will listen. Just because you have baggage doesn't mean that you have to schlep it with you into every situation. Self-knowledge means that you understand where your vulnerabilities lie, and you can warn your date about them. So instead of attacking when he bumps smack-dab into a sore spot, you can gingerly say, "Oops, sorry—that area's a particularly difficult one for me." You can also accept where his might lie. With this reasoning, it becomes easier to understand and accept that your date might also be harboring nasty little low-flying insecurities, which will allow a polite and sensitive, "Did I just walk into an area that's difficult for you?" when he seems to have overreacted. Neither of you are then forced to consider each other insensitive, nutty, or hysterical.

There are no such things in this life as overreactions. If you feel that either of you are overreacting, you're just missing a piece of the puzzle. If you're secure in yourself, you can be curious rather than furious in an unclear or confusing situation. If you're insecure, then in times of doubt you're going to be tempted to either attack or withdraw because it allows you to escape the necessity of defending yourself.

7. Criticism

Always criticize freely. If there's something you don't like, let people know—frequently, specifically, loudly and clearly, and, if at all possible, publicly . . . especially in front of your nearest and dearest. Anything is worth picking apart, literally, from top to bottom: haircuts, facial surgery, clothing, posture, musculature (or lack thereof), footwear, manners, driving acumen, physical clumsiness, or conversational skills. Do be sure that you correct any grammatical mistakes your date may make, including mispronunciations or misused foreign terms. And if he's polite enough to open doors for you, tell him that you're a liberated person who's perfectly capable; if he doesn't, stand there staring until he comes around (same goes for helping you with your coat). If possible, carry an umbrella—because nobody, except Hollywood, has figured out how to share an umbrella gracefully.

— **Avoiding disasters:** Criticism must be considered social dynamite and, as such, should be handled gingerly. When in doubt, instead of saying, "That's really stupid," try, "I must admit that this is an area that's particularly difficult for me. If you could try being on time, or if you could say that with slightly less volume, I'll be much less defensive." Saying, "I feel" rather than "You are," is a much more effective way of relating insecurities and communicating in general as opposed to either feeling like you're attacking or being attacked. (And no fair saying, "I feel you're a jerk!")

8. Jealousy

All of us would just as soon get what we want when we want it. The question is: How far are *you* willing to go to do so? If the sky's the limit, then jealousy is definitely your weapon of choice. You can cement your control by pointing out that no one has ever, can ever, or will ever appreciate, love, care for, or deserve your date more than you do. He's the coolest, sexiest, best-looking guy in the world, making you feel something you've never felt before. Tell him that you want to spend every moment with him, getting to know the real him. (And add that you're really sad you didn't get to know him as a child.)

If he's used to being ignored or having to compete for time—or he assumes that anyone whom he likes is never interested in him, is always too busy, or is commitment phobic—then you're golden, appealing, and seductive because you want to be with him all the time. Wait outside his house for him to come home, and call him a gazillion times a day to inquire where he is at every moment, as well as what he's wearing and doing. Check the mileage on his car and "accidentally" monitor his e-mail accounts, cell-phone speed dial, and bills. Being so enthralled will make *him* enthralled.

If your target (sorry—*date*) questions your enchantment as being less about him and more about your being a stalker in training, he's just not used to your brand of loving. Tell him that you can't let him out of your sight because everyone else will want him. Advise him on wardrobe and hairstyle choices, which will prove your love. Choosing scents, shoes, restaurants, music, movies, and style for him is about love and concern, which will deftly and slyly, not to mention subtly, allow you to take the next small step: advising him when, where, and what friends are allowed by convincingly pointing out that time spent with each other is the best time. Any resistance can be countered by pointing out that you want to spend all your time together, so why doesn't he feel the same? Explain to him that all you want is for the two of you to be your own tiny little universe, focused exclusively on one another.

— **Avoiding disasters:** While it may seem loving and appealing that someone could care so much initially, jealousy is the hallmark of someone who feels incompetent and therefore needs to make sure that your world is very circumscribed, limited, and scary. Consequently, the jealous party casts him- or herself as savior and protector. In the beginning of a relationship, this can seem very appealing, but it will soon become terrifying and claustrophobic.

In some ways, such controlling behavior is a character defect, but it's also the ultimate statement of insecurity. You're going to feel jealous if you think that someone can take something that you want away from you, and you'll never get it back. If that little green monster is bothering you, first ask yourself: Is it real or is it Memorex? In other words, is this an individual instance or a familiar pattern? If this isn't the first time you've felt this way, then it's time to tackle your own insecurities in either your choice of companions or situations, because otherwise there will be no such thing as a situation or individual that's reassuring enough to comfort you. You'll carry this burden around with you and poison every relationship, so you'll live out the following self-fulfilling prophecy: "Sooner or later, everyone will disappoint me, let me down, and eventually leave me." You'll *make* them leave you because of your jealousy.

If the green-eyed monster is new to you, understand that novels, TV, and movies have all taught us that making somebody jealous is a way of making them commit, making them appreciate our true worth by demonstrating that others love us or find us desirable. This behavior is neither cute nor

moral, appropriate nor adult—it's manipulative, shortsighted, and dangerous. If you feel jealous, you need to take a step back and look at what part
of your insecurities are being played on. Most often, jealousy is a pattern we
learn early on, which says that no one will ever love us, so it's only a matter of time until someone else takes what we really want. Don't use it, succumb to it, value it, or allow it.

9. Pretense

Reality is a waste of time—instead, create the perfect fantasy self: ide-
alized, desirable, a dream date come true from the get-go. A lie, you say?
Well, maybe . . . but *lie* is such a harsh word.

When in doubt, pretend, pretend, pretend. The lies—er—*fantasies* can
include (but not be limited to) your age, your weight, your sexual history,
even the gender you've always wanted to be. The Internet has made all this
not only possible, but an art form. And don't worry about the face-to-face
stuff—we humans see and believe what we want to. The more involved the
pretense, the easier it is to keep inflated: sexual preferences, what your parents do for a living, your educational background, your income, the cars you
own, where you live, how many people you've dated, whom you've had sex
with (along with the particular positions and locations), where you've traveled, who your friends are, what your résumé looks like, the pets you have,
why you have your lawyer's and/or bail bondsman's phone number on your

speed dial, how long you've been living at your current address, your country of origin, your politics, your religion, your shoe size, how many languages you speak, and how many brothers and sisters you have are all worth making up. Don't be intimidated by the fact that you barely know this person—he'll never remember it anyway, so become whom you'd like to be or think your date would like you to be.

Finally, keep in mind that it's okay to put some effort into being a nightmare. If it's too much trouble to make something up, be your real worst self up front by being as negative as you can: Bad-mouth everyone you can think of—your ex, your roomie, your family, your boss, the government—complain, whine, and test your date's capacity for sympathy. If he can accept the lousy you, just think how well the lovely you will work out!

— **Avoiding disasters:** If we were talking about a Miss America pageant, fund-raising, or trying to convince someone to give you a ride from work as a one-shot deal, then being the person you think they want you to be might be a worthwhile investment. However, we're talking about relationships here, so if you pretend from early on, when will it stop? If a man falls in love with the lie, then when you change, he's going to assume that if you pretended about one thing, you must have done so about others. You're really going to sabotage the relationship, and you're going to lose him. Pretending that you're always charming, or that you like things that you don't really like, means that one day you'll say, "I don't really like this," and the other person's going to say, "Well, why didn't you say something before?" Very good question.

Now, being your worst self may seem to have some inherent logic: "If he's seen the worst part of me, then he'll really love me when I stop doing this." The problem is that you're probably not going to have an audience by the time you've decided to become your nice self. Most people won't stick around for that kind of nonsense. If they do, then they're probably somewhat masochistic—and do you really want to be in a relationship with a masochist?

It's easy to get in the habit of being hypocritical and negative—but all you have to do if you never have anything nice to say about anyone else is decide that you're going to try to be positive for 24 hours. Conversely, if you're one of those people who's "always cheerful," try being honest for 24 hours and see how it changes your worldview. And if you constantly bad-mouth other people, you can make a deal with a friend that every time you say something negative, you give him or her $20. That'll change your habit really quickly!

Conclusions

There are many reasons why we date. Presumably, it can be for love, sex, fun, security, companionship, or arm candy; or it can be the desire for marriage and kids. So part of what you need to decide is your purpose for dating—not why someone else may be dating you, but why you're involved in this experience to begin with—because it will make a difference when it comes to whom you choose and why you choose them. For example, if power is the main reason you're dating (that is, the willingness or need to exert control over someone emotionally, physically, or spiritually), then with all due respect, you need a therapist, not a date. You're a wounded and sick puppy. If the need for dominance is your primary motivation, put this book down, go take a long, hard look in the mirror, and let's start all over.

Don't misunderstand me: I'm not suggesting that there's only one right reason to date. We live in a country where we're allowed to go out with someone without necessarily having an agenda—it may just be for the fun or socialization of it. But getting involved in a power struggle is going to truly create a disaster, and the easiest way of avoiding that is to avoid the assumption that everybody has the same purpose for dating. Instead, figuring out your own purpose for dating is really important, and then finding out your date's agenda makes a huge amount of sense as well.

Once you truly and specifically know your own desires, you can begin to inquire as to your date's agenda (maybe not on the first outing, but as soon as both of you begin feeling safe enough with each other to talk about what's important to each of you). This is as good a definition of intimacy as any. Realize, however, that some people are intimacy junkies (most of them are called "women"), so before launching yourself into the dating world, it's critical to know what it means to you. For many men, *intimacy* is synonymous with *sex,* while to many a female, it's the ability to talk and share. While there may be some overlap in these philosophies, they're obviously not the same kind of behaviors, and they imply very different kinds of techniques and motives.

In order to move from the status of strangers to anything more, from e-mailing to a coffee date, there has to be a willingness to be vulnerable, to let down some of the defense mechanisms and façade that we keep in place to keep ourselves safe. "I'll show you mine if you show me yours" isn't about genitalia, it's about heart, soul, identity, insecurities, strengths, and nutty family backgrounds. To go out with someone, sooner or later you've got to be willing to show who you really and what you really want, not exclusive of your warts and zits but inclusive of them, without resorting to power tools to keep you safe.

Of course, you'll need a secure place to stand, from which you feel strong, competent, confident, and willing to let someone else see who you really are. Once that's established, you can accept yourself, allowing yourself to take chances, be vulnerable, and attempt different behaviors because both strengths and weaknesses are known and accepted.

(**Author's note:** *For those of you who already know me, you know that the following experience was and is definitive of my sense of self—and my fear, risk-taking, and confidence. I beg your indulgence in hearing it again, or you can just skip this story. For the rest of you, onward.*)

When I first moved to New York, I didn't know anybody, I was working nights and weekends, and my salary went down by 50 percent while my cost of living doubled. As an adult, to have basically one quarter of what you had to live on the week before is alarming to say the least. So I did what I always do when I move to a new place: I walked around a lot, trying to get my bearings, and I found a place to work out. I figured that even if my life was chaotic, at least I could control my body to a certain extent. (Since I don't have the soul of an anorexic, controlling my body by purging and bingeing isn't my style—although I probably could've saved some money that way. Working out is my security blanket of choice.)

With my luck, I found the place where Mikhail Baryshnikov trained. I ended up sweating with all these little 19-year-olds who could take their left leg and wrap it twice around their heads without breaking a sweat. I felt like the elephant from *Fantasia* in my tutu. Anyway, I'd stand in the back of the class and think, *Okay, at least I have a Ph.D. To hell with them.* Now you could ask yourself, with great perception and an incredible degree of logic, "What does a Ph.D. have to do with working out?" And the answer would be a resounding, "Nothing!" But knowing that I had one gave me a safe place to stand so that I could literally be in that class, feeling like an uncoordinated blimp, but continuing to persevere. I thought, *I can define myself in terms of something positive (my Ph.D.) rather than something negative (my klutziness).*

Okay, my need to feel superior on some level at that moment probably doesn't say good things about me, but the truth is that I needed some kind of comfort that there was something I could do, and could do well, as opposed to these little nimble, skinny kids who were making me feel like a whale. Yes, I'm whining, but you get my drift.

You may be wondering why, if this book is about disasters, I'm talking about strengths. Well, if nothing else, the best way to doom your dating career is to start off by feeling really lousy about yourself. You'll be so consumed by your own misery and neediness that you'll be oblivious to any warning signs that another person is emitting.

The point is that in a relationship, unless you feel like Jabba the Hut, you must find and remind yourself about something about you that works. (Or conversely, to be maximally miserable, remind yourself repeatedly and constantly of your failures and shortcomings, and grab the power tools from this chapter.)

Now, in Part III, I'd like to switch gears a bit and share some quick tips with you to finish up the job. Hence, the ten disastrous dating commandments!

PART III

Disastrous
Dating
Commandments

CHAPTER 9

Get Engaged on Groundhog Day

This is all about being perverse, or: "Believe in opposites and deny your own needs." You see, the more you dislike yourself, the more interested you're going to be in finding someone who's completely different from you, which is why dating while you're in crisis makes so much emotional sense— not only can you distract yourself from your current misery, but you can find a man who's so unlike you that he'll never have your problems and will there- fore be continually happy and love you forever. Conventional wisdom would define you as unhappy and unappealing, but ignore that and take a walk on the wild side! Show the world that its definition of love, romance, san- ity, appropriate behavior, sensitivity, and boundaries is something at which you can, and do, scoff. If the world says zig, you, my dear, can always say zag: If most have a turkey dinner with loved ones on Thanksgiving, you'll fast and avoid family commitments; if the Fourth of July is about patriotism, you'll burn the flag; and in matters of the heart, you'll do the unexpected.

Ignoring New Year's Eve, your beloved's birthday, and the anniversary of your first kiss, along with arranging to be out of town on the day that you met will all establish that you're an original. When it comes to gift giving, act out: If your partner is a romantic, make sure that it's a practical one—and if he's practical, get him something completely useless. If he's on a diet, give him chocolates; and flowers are perfect for the guy with hay fever! When in doubt, get his present from a yard sale, a discount store, or anywhere that it can't be exchanged.

Expectations are always about power, so if you succumb now, you're doomed. If it's either fish or cut bait, engagement now or never, pick the most unlikely, least romantic moment possible to show that, yeah, you're feeling the pressure, but you're not happy about it. Get engaged on Groundhog Day! This will prove that Punxsutawney Phil is your patron romantic saint, not Cupid, dammit! If your intended doesn't like it, well, it's who you are. If he loves you, then he'll love your timing.

— **Avoiding disasters:** If one of you is romantic and the other isn't, take heed. Given that Groundhog Day is never more than a few days away from Valentine's Day, the most traditionally romantic of all holidays, and just weeks away from New Year's Eve, if you've found someone who wants to get engaged on Groundhog Day, he's likely to commemorate the engagement by gifting you with a jar of jam and a ring from a box of Cracker Jack. If you're partial to romance novels, big hearts, red roses, and meaningful engagements, you should ask yourself if this is a person with whom you can live the rest of your life. If you cry at Julia Roberts movies or devour *Bride's* magazine, beware!

In the long run, the underlying philosophy that both of you hold dear will absolutely affect how you interact. You can always negotiate the specifics, but if he really loves sports and you think that they're a way of expressing aggression in a paternalistic society, there's going to be some trouble. Of course, opposites *can* attract and profitably interact if the issues are trivial, but if the amount, variety, and intensity of what you disagree on are major issues, sure, you'll attract . . . and then you're going to aggravate the daylights out of each other.

In the early stages of a relationship, differences can seem enchanting, but as I've previously mentioned, a relationship should be more like Velcro—that is, in order for it to stick, you want the most number of contacts possible. As the two of you move through life, there are going to be all sorts of things that you have to battle, so the more you have in common—be it romance, a love of sports or TV, or a shared energy level—the more stable the relationship will be. (This is one of the reasons why joint ethnic traditions or religious or political beliefs can really hold people together—it's something that both parties believe in strongly. An emotional component like this can help a couple weather the rough times.)

So while some of those dissimilarities in the early days may seem just adorable, in the long run, the more you have in common, the more stable the relationship is going to be.

CHAPTER 10
Believe in Soul Mates and Love at First Sight

One of the most difficult parts of dating is worrying that you may be wasting your time—the anxiety of wondering not only if this guy is worth the effort, but whether he might actually see through your carefully constructed façade and then dump you. To sidestep this roadblock to your complete and utter happiness, you can short-circuit the entire lengthy, time-consuming process of getting to know your date by assuming from the get-go that you know every single teensy-weensy thing about him because you (pick one):

- have met in a previous life
- are soul mates
- are two halves of the same whole
- are the male and female equivalent of the other . . .

. . . or some equally poetic (and gooey) version of the "Where have you been all my life? You're completely different from anyone I've ever met, yet exactly like me!" song and dance. In this way, you're spared the tedious task of getting to know another person. You get to skip analyzing and evaluating either of your behaviors, negotiating any differences, or even acknowledging that anything either of you do, want, or believe will ever need any explanation or clarification. This will also allow you to ease off on your communication skills because a soul mate will instantly know exactly what you want, need, or mean at any moment. Think of all the time and effort you'll save!

— **Avoiding disasters:** An assumption of love at first sight is based on too little information and too much intensity. Granted, there's absolutely nothing wrong with sexual attraction, but to sugarcoat it with notions of "forever" is asking for trouble. Attraction is terrific, for it can certainly make the world go 'round and hearts beat faster—along with being a great reason to look further, take risks, and stick around. But "love at first sight" is actually "lust with potential," and people make the damndest assumptions based on it. Nothing's wrong with lust or potential, but neither should be confused with love or knowledge.

It's unrealistic to assume that somewhere out there, there's one perfect person who exists just for you—to make your life complete—and you'll both know it when he comes along. I certainly like romantic movies as much as the next person, and I hope that, like me, you don't confuse Hollywood with the real world. *Another person cannot complete you.* Relationships can't be the Spackle to your emotional drywall—you've got to be able to stand alone, comfortably and happily, before you can even think about being with someone else. That other person then has a manageable task: to merely add pleasure to an already functional and meaningful life.

This soul-mate business is really, really seductive because it's a chance to love ourselves while seeming to love someone else. We can simultaneously affirm that we're worthy of love while seeming to love another who—golly!—is just like us. Unfortunately, the price of this twofer is turning a blind eye, a deaf ear, and an ignorant heart to reality. Sooner or later, the discrepancies will begin to emerge. How long can a relationship exist based on who you'd like that person to be rather than who he *is?* How long can either of you ignore the differences that make each of you unique? If the similarities have been inflated to near-mythical proportions, then the differences are going to feel uncomfortable, and threaten to the illusion of compatibility you've created.

Now no one ever talks about taking a job or going on a vacation without doing some research. Even when we fall in love with a car, we have the mechanic check it out before we buy it. If it's a house, we wait for the bank appraisal before committing ourselves. And most women wouldn't even think of buying a dress or a pair of shoes without trying them on, doing some comparison shopping, or getting a friend's evaluation. It's only when our heart is at risk that we're so frivolous and daring. Only when it comes to love, the most important of all areas, do we embrace the notion of letting go and falling over the cliff. If you wouldn't close your eyes and jump in any other areas of your life that are much less life affecting than choosing a mate, then don't be so hasty when it comes to love.

That's the whole point of this book. On the one hand, you must be aware of what's going on, but on the other, you shouldn't make assumptions based on too little information. The only soul you'll ever truly know is your own, so believing in a soul mate when it comes to relationships is just plain stupid. What you want is enough similarity that the two of you have some activities in common, and you can share your partner's worldview in something that's already appealing to you. For example, if both of you really love travel, then that's something that may enhance the relationship.

The notion that both of you have to enjoy exactly the same things isn't accurate. So believe, up front, that there will be differences, and don't view them as threatening. Look for them, actively seek them out, enjoy them, and be curious rather than furious when you find them. After all, that's part of the fun of a relationship!

CHAPTER 11

Invest Heavily in the Beginning

Immediately jumping into a relationship with both feet will definitely give you that bungee-jumping, stomach-dropping, heart-stopping thrill that we all seek. You can proceed directly from first meeting to sex, and then to commitment, future planning, public statements (and public displays of affection), heavy financial involvement, and shared real estate; and introductions to co-workers, roommates, parents, miscellaneous relatives, exes, kids, the clergy, the post office, and the IRS.

Joint financial, emotional, medical, agricultural, and political endeavors should be sought out, immersed in, relished, and rehashed. The fact that you've spent more time researching your Palm Pilot than your partner should only make you believe in the difference between love and anything else on the planet. Doing what has worked for you in the past is fuddy-duddy thinking, and those who urge caution are jealous, jaded, or joyless.

— **Avoiding disasters:** Be very careful about assumptions, especially early on in a relationship, and be wary of investing too much too soon. There are a number of ways of investing—first is emotionally. Women, listen up here: Beware of calling your mom or your best friend after you've had a successful first date and projecting your future life with this man in great detail. Waxing rhapsodic about the dude while picking out the color of the bridesmaids' dresses or the kids' names is behavior that serves as a premature commitment based on essentially no information whatsoever (as well as being purely nutty); and the more you hear yourself talk, the more you'll believe that candy-coated dream scenario. Calling up Mom to say, "I've just met your future son-in-law," or "I never have to go on another date again," are seemingly harmless treacheries—seductive, global, and comforting—that allow you to believe your own nonsense, but nonsense it is. There's no way to know that much about a person in such a short amount of time. It's going to take a while to really get to know them (usually from six to nine months).

Next there's the biological investment—getting pregnant—which is why men *and* women must practice safe sex. You don't want to have a relationship determined by an unwanted or a surprise pregnancy, because both of you will then worry for the rest of your lives, *If we had never gotten pregnant, would the two of us have stayed together?* That's a huge burden under which to labor, pun intended. The worst reason in the world to get married is because you're pregnant.

Then there's the financial investment: buying property, sharing the rent, or starting a business together. The worst reason to be living together is because one of you just lost your apartment or your job. There's the possibility of meeting his friends or family too soon, going on vacation too soon, and planning for the future too soon. There really needs to be an organic unfolding of your partnership.

When it comes to a long-term relationship, you should view it in the same way that you would any other major emotional investment in life. As I've already mentioned, most of us wouldn't buy a car without shopping around, taking some test drives, or looking in *Consumer Reports*. At the very least, we'd think about what color we liked or what upholstery was the most comfortable.

The idea of deciding that you're desperately in love with someone in the beginning is a way of not doing the research—and that's a recipe for disaster. Instead, view yourself as an emotional archaeologist, sifting through the clues and trying to find out the real message of the civilization you're investigating—who lives there and what the rules, mores, and customs are. Archaeologists deal with things that are already dead and buried, but as an *emotional* archaeologist, you'll be dealing with something that's ongoing and dynamic—and is going to be interacting with you. It's really important to look at the clues carefully as opposed to investing in them immediately. Don't *love* the clues, *look at* them.

(Also, see yourself as gathering information not only about this other person, but about yourself and how you respond to that information. If you can turn yourself into a student of the relationship by taking an emotional step back—and I'm not suggesting that you divorce yourself from it or just become an observer and not a participant—you'll profit from it immeasurably.)

CHAPTER 12

Meet a Man on a Plane
(Especially One That's Going Through Turbulence)

Troubled times cry out for stability, and the best way to feel grounded is by glomming on to another soul. Statements like "Any port in a storm" or "In the land of the blind, the one-eyed man is king," have been coined for a reason. That's because just as pressure can harden coal into a diamond, rotten things in life can make us forget our usual constraints (and restraints). We can then feel free to grab on to whatever seems to be on the next trapeze if we feel ourselves falling through space. That repent-at-leisure stuff is just the voice of cynics who don't know the true meaning of love. Every country-western song ever written has gotten it right with the trinity of love: "I want ya, I need ya, I love ya."

— **Avoiding disasters:** Beware of situations that create false intimacy: an airplane, any natural disaster, the hospital, or staying late at work to meet a deadline; because your best friend left town or got married; or because you got fired, graduated, or moved to a new city. Basically, anything that heightens your emotions will lower your threshold.

When I worked at the World Trade Center site following 9/11, I saw relationships blossom that I knew were going to have a very short half-life. That's because adrenaline is a great high, but sooner or later it dissipates or goes away, resulting in a very bad low. Heightened emotional situations make us feel needy and vulnerable, which then creates a false intimacy.

Since I've used the model of computer dating to describe the men in this book, let me take a moment to warn you about e-mailing. I have no problem with it for a short period of time, but sooner or later, you're going to have to meet that person face-to-face, and what you want is the most reliable information you can get. Now, I can already hear some of you arguing with me: "No, e-mail completely transcends chemistry and, therefore, people can be honest," but that's the whole point! It's a *false intimacy.* You don't really know this person, and if you wouldn't say all the things that you're saying over e-mail to a stranger at the supermarket, then you shouldn't be saying them to your cyber-buddy—who, in fact, is a stranger, too.

Understand that there are times in life when you're less capable of making good decisions. If you can't decide whether or not to get out of bed in the morning, then this really isn't the time to decide about a relationship, although it *is* when you may feel the most need for one. At those times, you're looking for some stability, but understand that whatever you find to give it to you externally will just be a crutch. You need to have *internal* stability—otherwise, you're going to have an artificial sense of needing the person. It's doubtful that he's going to like feeling like a crutch, since not only will you put all your weight on him, but when you recover your equilibrium, you're going to toss him aside. Nobody walks around with a cane or a crutch they don't need.

You need to take your own emotional pulse sometimes. The time that you should least be in a relationship is when you're feeling the neediest. If you're a white-knuckle flyer like me, meeting men in planes may have the ability to distract you from the life-threatening situation your stomach feels you could be in, but when that plane lands, you're going to have an emotional investment in a person whom you barely know. "Flying the friendly skies" is probably not a good idea for the long term.

CHAPTER 13

Assume That Sex Means Anything

When it comes to the question of following your head or your heart, the true romantics of this world understand that the feeling of being head-over-heels, over-the-moon crazy about someone is worth whatever the cost. Thinking is the enemy of passion and love, and just letting it all hang out would cure most of the world's ills (okay, maybe not overpopulation or AIDS, but basically everything else).

You've gotta just let go and get carried away, because the sex with your current flame is more amazing than what Diane Lane got from that French guy in *Unfaithful*. You connect so well sexually that you just know in your very soul that he's The One.

— **Avoiding disasters:** I know that most of you will take umbrage with me on this, but understand that sex increases hormones and, thus, heightens one's emotional state—which is going to reduce your ability to think things through. Anybody who has sex on the first date these days is just plain stupid—sure, we're all tempted to, but hopefully, our big fancy cortex that sits on top of all our other organs reminds us, "You don't know this person."

Now, I actually had a call recently from a 25-year-old man who'd gotten a 19-year-old pregnant on their first date. He was trying to get me to convince her to give the child up for adoption because he didn't want to be a father. Well, *hello!* If he didn't want to be a father, then he shouldn't have had sex with this girl, or at least he should have used a condom.

If I were the mother of a daughter (which I am), I'd say, "Never have sex with a man who refuses to use a condom. He has no respect for himself or you, and who knows who else he's talked into doing the same thing?" And if I were the mother of a son, I'd staple the ol' love glove on his whatchama-jiggy because until he's ready to be a father, the only way to make sure he'll take responsibility is if he doesn't have sex or doesn't have unprotected sex. Fellows, the days of, "Well, I don't know if it's mine," have come and gone. Can you say "DNA testing"?

Sex, even in these modern times, quite often means something completely different to men than it does to women. In a relationship, a man can use it for healing—to feel better about himself or his partner, or after an argument. For the woman, it's very likely, "I don't want to have sex with you until I'm healed." You see that both of these can be misinterpreted: The man may tell himself, "Okay, if we're having sex, then she's not mad at me anymore," while she may feel, "Well, if we're having sex, then he understands why I was mad at him." Neither is true.

The notion that men will trade intimacy for sex, while women will trade sex for intimacy, is probably truer than we'd like to think about in this day and age. When guys feel unhappy, alone, alienated, or sad, they can be quite seductive. Men aren't stupid (although women very often assume that they are)—most over the age of five have learned how to cloak some of their sexuality in more emotional terms that are acceptable to women. (Otherwise, they'd just masturbate all the time.) Similarly, for hundreds of years, women have had to rationalize their own sexuality into thinking it was something more.

Now gals are notoriously dense about assuming that because a man says "I love you" in bed, it really means anything. Both sex and love are perfectly nice, but *they're not the same thing.* Because the sex is good doesn't mean that two people have anything to talk about once the passion goes away; and if it isn't good, that doesn't necessarily mean that it can't be improved. (As to that age-old question about chemistry: In spite of Billy Crystal and Meg Ryan in *When Harry Met Sally,* the people who believe that it can be cultivated over time are called . . . women.)

The point of all this is: *Do not confuse sex with anything other than sex.* Even men will tell you that all orgasms aren't the same, and really caring about somebody makes the experience completely different. And for most women, unless there are some emotional feelings, sex doesn't tend to be so great. The thing to be very careful about here is assuming—and this is really an assumption that women make more than men—that if the sex is great, it must mean that you love each other. Don't buy it. Be careful about sex being symbolic of anything. It is what it is . . . and both of you need to be very clear about what it is for each of you. Make sure you both know it in your own heads and communicate it to each other.

CHAPTER 14
Count Condoms

While throwing yourself emotionally and physically into a relationship is part of the fun (see the previous chapter), trusting your partner is going to make you look like a fool—and the most you can hope for is to catch him before he cheats on you. So throw your body but not your trusting soul into the mix here.

Don't be misled by seeming innocence or full disclosure on your partner's part: The guiltiest always look the most honest. Always ask for details of past relationships; even if there have been no indiscretions, the odds are that sooner or later . . . well, you get the point. Be ever vigilant, including checking e-mails, cell phone bills, wallets, and diaries; go through drawers, cabinets, and closets; and assume that if you don't find anything, he's just hiding it really well. Above all, keep track of anything on and in nightstands. After all, anybody who doesn't keep a condom count is deserving of whatever she gets.

— Avoiding disasters: If you can't trust the man you're with, it's either thanks to your paranoia or his untrustworthiness. If you're going through his wallet, briefcase, or Palm Pilot; checking his e-mails or cell phone bills; or rifling through his medicine cabinet to see if the number of condoms he has matches your last count, you either need a therapist or a new guy. Such activity—along with following his car and dropping in unexpectedly—are all attempts at "Gotcha!" behavior, and it's contemptible and stomach turning. Either you trust the guy or you don't—if you don't, then either talk about it or walk. Counting condoms is a way of making yourself nuts.

I actually had a call from a woman who told me, "I've been married for three months. My husband is a good-looking lawyer, and women are always coming on to him. Should I trust him?"

"Why is he telling you all these things?" I wondered. "It's really inappropriate." And she said, "Because I ask and I want to know." I retorted, "Honey, then you set it up. He doesn't know what the right answer to the question is. If you ask him, 'Do other women find you attractive?' and he says no, he worries about whether *you* find him attractive, or if you'll only think he's attractive if other women find him so. If he says yes, he then worries that you don't trust him. Stop asking stupid questions."

Either you trust or you don't. If the two of you were drawn to each other because of physical attraction to begin with, which is perfectly okay with me, then being threatened by the fact that you're both attractive people is stupid. And asking someone to be dishonest isn't a very smart thing to do.

Finally, keep in mind that most people are pretty trustworthy . . . until they feel that somebody doesn't trust them. At which point, they usually figure, *The hell with it—if she [or he] doesn't trust me in the first place, then why bother?* Snoops don't sleep well at night.

CHAPTER 15
Date Outside Your Area Code

Nothing contributes more to that sense of mystery and romance than distance. Vacation sex is synonymous with romance and passion, and meeting each other in strange places or while visiting friends or relatives gives both of you the sense of how inconvenient you can really be. The fantasy aspect, the longing, and the ignorance of what your real lives are like will keep the fire burning a lot longer than that day-to-day nonsense.

"Same time, next year" means that if the two of you remain strangers, the sex will stay hot, and the commitment will be driven by what you *might* have rather than what you *actually* have. In fact, really getting to know a man should *only* happen after the two of you have already totally committed to one another—that is, after you've moved in with him and given up your lease; gotten pregnant; or left a long-term relationship, job, or favorite pet!

— **Avoiding disasters:** When thinking about the issue of trust, consider the fact that I've actually known men who've told me with an absolutely straight face that extramarital dalliances are okay, "As long as my wife doesn't know about it," "As long it doesn't mean anything," "As long as I still love my wife," or my personal favorite, "As long as it's more than a 25-mile radius away from home," then it "really doesn't count." This brings us to never dating outside your area code.

What this means is that you're going to spend a lot of time apart, and while it's sometimes necessary for couples to be away from each other for a while, the idea of launching a relationship when you don't even live near each other is just plain nutty. It's perfectly okay to be friends—and I suppose if you're into vacation sex, you can do that, too, but I certainly wouldn't treat it as a real relationship.

A long-distance relationship only works well in the movies because it's primarily a fantasy. You're going to spend so much more time apart than together that you're not going to know who that person truly is . . . and that's the whole point of this book. You've gotta know who you are, and you've gotta know who this other person is. As I've mentioned many times, dating is the process of getting to know somebody *slowly* and *carefully*. After the initial attraction, you'll want to see what it's like to be around this person on an ongoing basis. You'll want to spend time together so that your relationship can grow organically. If the two of you are forced to condense things because of geographical constraints, then the combination of attraction and time pressure is going to tempt you to be sexual before you really have the chance to know each other.

Let's say for a moment that you're heterosexual and you hit it off with someone of the same sex at a party. You might say, "Hey, would you like to have a cup of coffee next week?" And assuming that the two of you had a great time, you might say, "Gee, this was really great . . . we should do it more often. Do you want to go shopping, catch a baseball game, or grab a drink?" Over time, the two of you, slowly and carefully—and without disrupting your lives or jettisoning other relationships—would begin to see how much you had in common and enjoyed each other's company. Assuming that every experience was more positive and better than the last, you wouldn't be considered foolish to want to spend more time together.

Now if we add sex into the mix (you can now envision replacing your platonic friend with a hottie of the opposite sex), there's going to be a natural urgency that your body will feel because that's how bodies are meant to respond sexually. You want to keep those impulses under enough control so that your more logical self can evaluate rather than just respond and be swept away. You need to try to balance that urgency with information that's received over a period of time. You want to see this person in his natural habitat . . . in order to do that, you have to know what his natural habitat is. If the two of you live in completely different time zones, how are you really ever going to know anything about him?

~~~ ~~~

If I were in charge of dating, everyone would wear old (but clean) clothes on a first date, women wouldn't shave their legs, men wouldn't shave their faces, both would have fresh breath, and they'd go take a walk in the park. The idea is that they'd observe each other in a nonstressful situation so that they didn't make assumptions based on the anxiety of the situation, which will distort perception.

I'm reminded of this experiment that was done back when fraternities and sororities were a big deal, hazing was part of the rush procedure, and women were still uncomfortable about being considered uncouth or un-ladylike (definitely pre-Britney Spears and *Sex and the City*). Three groups of women were told that they were being rushed for a sorority that required an initiation. All three groups were told that they were being tested on how fast and accurate they could take dictation.

The first group sat with a woman who read neutral words like *cat* and *dog;* the second had a man reading similar neutral words; and the third had a man reading obscene, four-letter words. When questioned afterward on their feelings about the sorority, the first group thought that the whole thing was stupid—they didn't see what the fuss was about and would never join that sorority. The second was slightly more interested in pledging, but the third uniformly thought that the sorority was fabulous! They'd pledge *and* recommend it to their friends.

The researcher's conclusion was that the more struggle, emotion, and anxiety attached to something, the more likely we'd be to assess that experience as being worthwhile. When we take the paradigm and apply it to dating, that means that the more hassle involved in getting together, the more we're going to value the experience. So the idea is that you want as little hassle as possible.

Long distance means that every time the two of you get together, it's a hassle. Dating the boy next door is an old-fashioned notion, but it means that you both have something in common, and it's not very hard to bump into each other.

Now do I think dating the boy next door is a good idea? No. If something goes wrong, you're going to start spying on one another—you don't want the whole neighborhood watching you at all times, and you also don't want to be in something purely for convenience. However, you *do* want to be in a relationship where the two of you are at least in the same time zone so you can get to know each other without a huge amount of fuss, fantasy, or rationalization involved.

CHAPTER 16
Give a Man a Cow
(Overwhelm Him)

If you can overwhelm a man, he'll be off balance, which means that you can control the relationship and things will go and be as you wish them to. Your guy may respond by trying to outdo you, but hey, who says competition has to be a bad thing in a relationship? Winning can be fun! And while most folks aren't crazy about losing, if you can keep your fella on his toes, he may not even realize that he lost. He'll then cling to and need you, so you'll get yourself some job security—especially if you can convince him that nobody can do as well, as often, or as lavishly as you. And if he ever doubts it, you can certainly remind him, chapter and verse.

— **Avoiding disasters:** I must confess that this commandment stems from a personal story, even though I'm a city person and, in theory, so was this guy I was dating. Actually, he was a city boy who played gentleman farmer on the weekends. One such weekend, while we were on the way to a farm-implement auction, he spent eight hours and hundreds of miles obsessing about a combine or something that he *hadn't* bought for $75 to use for spare parts. The next weekend, I was primed and ready.

We set off for a livestock auction, where he spied a cow that he loved. Unfortunately, he was outbid, but I was unprepared to hear about it for more hours and miles. So I went to the office to find out who bought the cute bovine and for how much. The lady in the office recognized me and asked what I could possibly want with a cow in the city.

I responded, "If people can have Great Danes, why can't I have a cow?"

She was convinced that I was serious and earnestly tried to point out the pooper-scooper problem, bless her heart. I should also mention that the guy in question's birthday was merely days away, and how often do you know exactly what to get the man who has everything?

Armed with information and resolve, I tracked down the surprised and suspicious John Deere hat–wearing owner of said cute bovine, who told me that he'd only sell her if he could make a profit on the cow he'd owned for the last 15 minutes. My heart sank, but I asked him how much, and he said that he'd have to make at least $25. Done deal! I was now the proud owner of the perfect birthday present—except nothing was ever the same again, and it had nothing to do with cow patties.

The problem was that not only had I invaded my date's turf, but he had no way to respond in kind—let alone top me. My seemingly good deed did not go unpunished.

(**Author's update:** *My cow not only won several competitions, but eventually produced ribbon-winning offspring. I wonder if that makes me a bovine granny?*)

Men fall into two categories: those who are really good at gift giving, and those who aren't, and neither one will be pleased by a cow. If he prides himself on his skills with a present, you've just moved the bar impossibly high. *What fun,* you're thinking, but you must realize that *he's* the one who comes up with cool ideas to stun, amaze, and delight you. He gets to preen, and your job is to "Ooh" and "Aah". And if he's not good at gift giving, well, it's not like he's going to learn from example.

So what should you do—not in terms of livestock, but gift giving? Well, keep in mind the basic tenets of any relationship: balance, expectation, and most important, a willingness not to compete. As women work, age, and prosper, the role of cheerleader, second-stringer, or docile child becomes less and less attractive. Instead, it's replaced by a desire to be taken seriously while playing with the big boys. Gift giving is an area where less is going to be more for a long time to come, since it's about control, lifestyle, reciprocity, and all sorts of things that men have traditionally dominated. How can anybody top a cow? (Well, yeah, you're right, a horse would be a good start . . . but you get my point.)

What you want to do is leave something for later to show the guy who you really are. For a lot of people who are naturally generous, what they want to do is have the sense that they can give, and have it be reciprocated. But that, again, has to happen slowly and over time. A good rule of thumb is to ask yourself: "If he did for me what I'm about to do for him, would I feel overwhelmed?" And if the answer is yes, don't do it!

The notion that you can wow or dazzle someone so much that they'll fall in love with you is really a short-term solution to a long-term problem. At some point you're going to run out of dazzle—will the relationship go away? When he asks, "Wait a minute, don't you love me anymore?" and you say, "Well, don't you love *just* me without the presents?" . . . well, how could he, when he never got to know the real you? You were always trying to impress him. So while on some level dazzling can be construed as generosity, it's really a statement of insecurity.

A generous impulse is good, but a thoughtful analysis is better. So beware of overdoing it: You may be trying to compensate for something lurking just below the surface of your psyche—possibly the need to please or overwhelm him, or to show him how to do it right.

Part of what we all of want to do in a relationship is to let the other person see through the façade and understand who we really are. No one wants to feel as if they're being taken advantage of or being used, and I think that men are especially anxious about this. They worry that women are just going out with them because they're desperate and hear their biological clock ticking, they want a free dinner, or they like the way the men dress or dance. We women, on the other hand, are concerned about men wanting to date us because we're good arm candy or breeding material, because they're lonely and need a date for a wedding, or because they just want sex. So we all come to the dating table with a boatload of expectations and maybe a little bit of baggage here and there.

One of my real revelations as an adult was understanding that I could go to a party without taking a gift, tending bar, passing hors d'oeuvres, or staying to clean up—in other words, I was really invited because the host wanted to have me there. It wasn't that he or she was making the problem for me, I was making the problem for myself. To a certain extent, this is the same thing with dazzling. It's a statement of insecurity, and it's unnecessary . . . unless, of course, you really do want a disaster on your hands.

CHAPTER 17

Lie about the
Small Things

There are things from your past that you're not crazy about: stuff you might want to change but haven't quite gotten around to yet; issues you've thought about tackling in therapy or have heard about from friends, lovers, and family members for years. Never mind—you can ignore them all, especially if you want someone to love and value you. So when in doubt, exaggerate, lie, finesse, tease, obscure, or pretend that you didn't understand your beloved's question.

If you've been prepared for these sensitive areas thanks to past experiences, why not have a whopper prepared in advance? The fact that you haven't gotten away with it before should in no way deter you. It's also never a bad idea to stay in lying shape, so fib even when the stakes are low or non-existent.

That's right—don't limit yourself to the important stuff! Lie about where you're going or what you're doing, what you're eating or thinking, and whom you know, love, or hate. You can name-drop a name, place, or situation; and creativity is much to be valued. Don't worry about getting caught—if you do, you can simply come up with another lie, spirited defense, distraction, accusation, or sheepish grin. And keeping track of who you've told what to is probably not worth the effort.

— **Avoiding disasters:** Between honesty and duplicity is silence, and certainly early on in a relationship, it's perfectly okay to say nothing. It someone asks, "How old are you?" rather than telling a lie, it's perfectly acceptable to say, "No true gentleman would ever ask a lady such a question, sir." My way of dealing with that issue is just to explain that everyone in my family is 29. It's a genetic predisposition: "My grandmother's 29, my mom's 29, all my aunts and sisters are 29, and my daughter's 29. But we all look much older than 29, and we're all very sensitive about it." That's a way of politely saying, "How dare you ask my age!"

In theory, the three things that everybody is allowed to lie about are their age, their weight, and their sexual history, but rather than doing so, it's probably better to just finesse it and refuse to answer at all. Income or anything to do with money can also be included here—just because someone's rude enough to ask doesn't mean that you have to be foolish enough to answer. The point is: When in doubt, instead of lying, all you have to say is absolutely nothing. You'll save yourself a lot of wear and tear in the long run.

Now, lies that are hard to recover from, like those concerning previous marriages, children, bankruptcies, or jail sentences, should be avoided altogether. While you may legitimately feel that nobody has a right to ask those questions on a first date, who wants to confide in a stranger? But it's sometimes difficult to determine just when a stranger becomes someone with whom you're willing to invest emotionally. When is it going to be okay to go back and revise those initial statements? The answer is: There's very seldom a good time. Big lies are nearly impossible to set right, but even little ones can cause the "If somebody would lie about something inconsequential, what else would they lie about?" blues. Lying really is a trap.

Let me give you an example from my own life of what I mean. I had the experience once in medical school of trying to help a guy who had a damaged windshield. We were in Massachusetts at the time, and you needed to get a sticker to get your car to pass inspection. He didn't have the money to get his windshield replaced, yet he'd done me the enormous favor of tutoring me through biochemistry. When he told me that his car wouldn't pass, in a moment of true naivete, I responded, "I think you can buy those stickers."

What this sparked was a real odyssey through the dark underbelly of the world. I ended up talking to people who had been "sent up the river" (prison) to try to find this guy a car sticker. For the first time in my life, I had great sympathy with Richard Nixon because I understood that once you start one lie, you have to continue.

When the first person I called to ask, "Hi! I have a friend who won't pass inspection, so I was wondering where can I get an illegal inspection sticker?" hung up on me, I learned to be creative. At one point I was so good at making up these lies that I ended up with two stickers. However, I was so uncomfortable about it that I was convinced I'd be in a car accident, the police would find these on me, and my soul would go to hell.

It's very hard for all of us to tell the truth all the time, especially when we live in a country that supports lying. We have television programs in which the whole premise is false, whether it's that this slob is somebody I really want to marry and if I can convince my family, I'll get a million dollars; or I'm really a millionaire, but I'm pretending not to be so that I can tell if you really love me; or I'm really not a millionaire, but I play one on TV; or I really do love you, but too bad—I'm just in it for a television contract. But what your mother told you is right: Lying is not a good idea. You're going to get caught, especially if you don't have a poker face. And if you're ever in doubt, just don't say anything at all.

CHAPTER 18

Assume That You Can Change Him

Y ou know you're not perfect, even though you go out of your way to make sure that no one finds this out. But that shouldn't stop you from performing a top-to-bottom, inside-out makeover on your man. Even though you know how hard change is for you, it's a lot easier for your partner, since he has you—and if he truly loves you, he'll want you to be *really* happy. After all, love conquers all!

— **Avoiding disasters:** Men get involved with women assuming that they'll never change, while women get involved with men assuming that they can change them—that guys are somehow raw material. This only serves to make everyone unhappy. He is who he is; it's not that the two of you can't negotiate with one another, but assuming that there are going to be massive changes in personality or behavior is just a way of making you both maximally miserable.

Potential is one of the nastiest words in the English language. Thinking that you're going to make this man somebody he's not is poisonous to you both. If you can't accept who he is, drop him and move on. It's amazing how many women decide, once they're married, to morph somehow from his cute little love bunny into his mother. They resolve to be in charge of his vices, his work, his relationship with his parents and his friends, how he treats the children, and how he does the housework.

Understand that a mother may be a lot of things, but sexy she's not—and the more you become your partner's mom, the more he'll become the naughty little boy who tries to break the rules or get away with something. He'll become uncommunicative and less than honest. Remember when your mother asked you where you were going? You'd say, "Out," and that what you were doing was "Nothing." That's not the role you want in either a marriage or a loving relationship.

Underwear can be changed, diapers can be changed, addresses can be changed, but people change *themselves* or they don't change at all. If you assume that your partner already is who he's going to be, you're going to be a lot better off. That's why it's so important to know this guy well, to move carefully, and not to let hormones color your vision. You need to see each other under normal circumstances, not make assumptions up front, and be as honest as you possibly can so that he's honest in return. There's no sense in pretending to be a banana if you're really an orange.

Don't assume that you're going to change anybody—or even that they're going to change themselves. And turning into somebody's parent is a very bad idea. And if you start forgetting this point, just remind yourself how you treat your own mother when she tries to tell you what to do. . . .

IN CLOSING

You've undoubtedly noticed the somewhat tongue-in-cheek tone of this book, in which I've facetiously implied that disastrous dating is accomplished by either scouting out lunatics or discovering your own inner lunatic. Hopefully you've figured out that a lot of the "all men [or women] behave badly" party line is a great deal less than serious; meant to be fun, silly, entertaining, and eventually enlightening; and that what's ultimately important is self-evaluation. We live in a society where it's very easy to blame others, and the sexes continually battle each other. From my perspective as a psychologist, men and women seem angrier and less accepting of each other's foibles right now than at any other time I can remember.

Yet despite this clear antagonism, there's still a basic wish and need to put together a viable personal relationship. The notion that all men are either married, gay, or Mama's boys isn't a fair way of looking at them. And men viewing all women as castrating witches (with a capital "B") is equally unfair. So how do you actually make a healthy, fulfilling, and positive relationship with somebody work? As you've probably already sorted out by reading this book, *you* are as crucial to the equation as the other person—you've got to know who you are and what you want first and foremost. The more you know yourself, the more you can present yourself honestly and understand what parts of *you* need to change.

I often ask callers to my radio show to write a painfully honest personal ad for themselves, including the three major things they like about themselves and three things they hate. This may benefit you as well, since you may find that the things you don't like may actually appeal to another person. For example, if you feel that you talk a lot, then someone who considers himself a good listener might think that you're just dandy. Your ad could then say, "Looking for a quiet, good listener who loves being entertained by me."

The second reason to write a personal ad for yourself is to be very specific about what you want. For example, if you have a lot of energy and want to find someone similar, make that clear. Don't say you want someone "like me," because how is anyone going to know who you are? Explain how your energy plays out, and the pleasures and the difficulties it presents.

Self-knowledge, in a very specific way, allows you to communicate clearly who you are, to actually like yourself (which is a crucial aspect for long-term dating), and to decrease the possibility that you're going to be insecure, jealous, or negative about other people or that you're going to pretend. If you can look at yourself unblushingly and without shame, and you can then give another person a clear idea of who you are, this allows for some real communication. By dovetailing who you are with what you want from someone else, a personal ad can become a very useful tool for both sides. Just keep repeating to yourself, "Be specific." Don't allow yourself to wander into the level of the trite or symbolic—no "long moonlit walks with a true soul mate" for you.

Another effective way to get to know yourself is to look at patterns in your own behavior. If you notice yourself picking the same person over and over again, you must ask yourself why you might be doing so. To say, "Well, I always pick the Dance-Away Lovers" is fine, but the question is: *Why* are you picking Dance-Away Lovers? Instead of looking for why you attract these types of people, ask yourself what attracts *you* to that type of relationship. (You may want to take a quick peek at my previous book, *Getting Unstuck,* for the specifics in identifying and changing destructive patterns.)

In addition to this practice, asking your best friend to be painfully honest with you is a great idea. (Think of all those thoughts that you've held back when she's told you for the 80th time that year that the guy hasn't called back. . . . If you can, have an "ollie ollie oxen free" and tell her exactly what's on your mind, being totally frank without brutally saying, "Has it ever occurred to you that you could make better choices?")

~~~ ~~~

Some very basic rules of thumb should have jumped out at you during the reading of this book, whether you were giggling, sighing, or sobbing. The first one is *take the time*. Whenever we rush to a conclusion in a relationship, we do ourselves an injustice. Most of us are horrifyingly susceptible to the Burger King–theory of life: We want it quick, hot, and our way, even if it takes two hands to handle it. But in relationships, there's no substitute for getting to know someone slowly and carefully over time—to allow for ripening, if you will. Dating is an attempt to balance two very basic, fundamental concerns: One is the sexual impulse, which is intended to be thoughtless and urgent; and the other is a wish for continuity, because we're human beings, not animals. Urgency doesn't serve long-term goals at all, and continuity requires experience over time in an orderly, if not predictable, fashion, which offers the possibility of trusting another and trustworthiness of self. So take the time.

I'm reminded of this old joke about a very sophisticated, handsome, accomplished diplomat who was being interviewed by a reporter. When asked why he'd never married, he answered, "Alas, I was looking for the perfect woman." The reporter said, "Well, isn't it too bad that you never found her." And he replied, "No, I did find her—unfortunately, she was looking for the perfect man."

The Human Genome Project has given us the mistaken notion that somehow everything about us is describable, knowable, and therefore eventually correctable, but genes are one thing—human behavior is a great deal more complex. We're each a compilation of our individual experiences (both the good and the bad), and we're like snowflakes: unique and different. This, in essence, is the pleasure of adult dating and adult life itself: understanding what it is about us that's like everyone else and what's completely unique.

As a psychologist, what continually fascinates me is how we confuse the two. You see, the things we don't like about ourselves are quite often the things that *nobody* likes about themselves. The fact that we can be petty, egocentric, or vindictive at times are all common human traits—sure, they're not laudable, but they're not horrifying either. The traits that make us uncomfortable or ashamed, like our whacked-out sense of humor or quirky way of eating an egg, or the fact that we tend to be overly generous with food at Christmastime, are probably the things that make us endearing, worthwhile, interesting, and valuable to others. Part of not only the dating experience but adult life in general is understanding the difference between what's normal and what's not, what's valuable and what's not, and what's common and what's not. Dating gives you an understanding of this that nothing else can because it's so intimate, intense, and one-on-one.

When a relationship goes well, it makes you very happy, but if it goes poorly, it becomes very destabilizing. Not only does it throw off the romantic, emotional part of your life, but it also upsets the balance across the board. You don't like your friends as much, you become whiny and discouraged, and feel a dislodged sense of self. While relationships certainly represent the peak of your emotional life and are worth investing in, making the same painful mistakes over and over has major ramifications in all the other aspects of your life.

In general, whether you're aware of it or not, what you want in a relationship at some point is the ability to relax and be yourself without stress or anxiety. I know that common wisdom dictates the wish for constant stimulation—that true love is all about making your stomach hurt and palms sweat—but that's confusing fear or lust with love. In other words, you're having an adrenaline response, which may be fun in the beginning, but certainly isn't sustainable over any period of time. Sanity dictates a comfort level in a relationship that allows you to experiment personally, socially, profession- ally, or perhaps even sexually so that you can grow and become a better per- son. Thanks to this stable basis with another person, you're allowed to feel like you're a little less alone and vulnerable. And knowing who you are, being able to present yourself honestly, and figuring out the important things in your life—including what's negotiable and what's not—make up the busi- ness of adult life.

~~~ ~~~

The last thing I want to emphasize is that even though this is a book about dating, it's perfectly okay to be alone. Until you can accept this, you're going to be much more at the whim of your emotions and needs than your wants. In the long run, a relationship will survive best and be the strongest if it's based on want and not need. There are all sorts of ways to get some of the emotional benefits commonly associated with dating from other kinds of relationships, including those with friends, family members, neighbors, co-workers, fellow members of your congregation or political party, and folks you meet while volunteering—all of which can make you feel connected and worthwhile.

If you put all your emotional eggs in the dating basket, you're going to have an awful lot of omelettes . . . and an awful lot of eggshells in those omelettes. You see, there may be times in your life when you've just suffered a broken heart, are going through a divorce, have suffered a loss, are diverted by work, are taking care of loved ones, or aren't feeling healthy—

again, the world's worst time to start dating is when you're feeling miserable. Dating is high-risk behavior, so you need to feel secure and happy to decide to launch into it. Ironically, this may encourage others to seek you out 'cause you're just so darned cute, well adjusted, attractive, and happy.

It's okay to take breaks from dating—or to decide that you're never going to date at all—because there are other ways to get the emotional goodies that dating can offer with somewhat less risky behavior. But when you do date, understand that it's a choice, not a necessity. You can offset any urgency that "this has to work out okay or I'll die!" by reminding yourself that dating is just a diversion, the cherry on an ice-cream sundae. Believe that when they lay you out for your last rattly little breath, if your heart doesn't have a couple scars and a bruise or two, you haven't taken nearly enough chances in this life.

So, date! But know that sooner or later, even if you're really good at it and have absorbed every single lesson of this book, there's still going to be a disaster or two waiting for you. *It's okay.* Go for it, believing in the myriad possibilities the world has to offer, as well as your own resiliency. There really is some alternative to disastrous dating and relationships, but remember: *You've got to play to win.*

Acknowledgments

Not so long ago, I was invited to the Algonquin for dinner, so wanting to be my most elegant Dorothy Parker-esque, I donned black stockings, black heels, a black leather mini (no comment, purists), and a black turtleneck with a fabulous art deco necklace . . . okay, so it was Dorothy Parker channeled through the Beat generation or something.

At any rate, the necklace was heavy and valuable, and while I could manage the clasp, the safety chain was beyond my abilities. Since I wanted to wow my date fully formed, when I got off the elevator, I cajoled five—count 'em, five!—guys to help me with the irritatingly small hook and clasp. A book is much the same situation. It took a village to get me lookin' good, and it takes similar efforts and personnel to do the same when it comes to the task of writing.

I sincerely and with heartfelt emotion thank the following:

Hay House Honchos:

- Reid Tracy—for helping me keep things on track and believing in this project.

- Danny Levin—for wise counsel and good humor.

- Jill Kramer—for helping me to appear at least semiliterate.

- Shannon Littrell—for polishing, cajoling, questioning, and making things better one more time.

- Christy Salinas—for making the cover *kaboom!*
- Louise Hay—for being the guru who inspires.

William Morris Mamas:

- Joni Evans—wise woman, moral supporter, critic, friend . . . who could ask for anything more?
- Sarah Pollard—fabulous Joni-in-training with an acute eye, a kind tongue, and an angelic temperament.

Home-Turf Builder:

- Kate Finney—couldn't have done it without ya, cookie! From your raised eyebrow to your smiling nods to your ability to discern my scrawl, you made this a much less lonely endeavor.

Y'all:

- You keep buyin' 'em, I'll keep writin' 'em. Thanks for your support, your trust, and your willingness to tell me what's really going on in your life.

And for those of you who have contributed personally—*very* personally—to the tone and content of this book, I thank you.

About the Author

Dr. Joy Browne is a licensed clinical psychologist and the host of her own internationally syndicated daily radio show. Every day, millions of listeners in the U.S., Canada, and on Armed Services Radio worldwide hear her give advice on everything from cheating boyfriends to the best new plays on Broadway. She has won numerous awards for her work, including the American Psychological Association's President's Award and the *TALKERS Magazine* award for Best Female Talk Show Host two years in a row. In addition to radio, Dr. Browne has hosted her own television show and has been a guest on *Oprah, Montel, Larry King Live,* and more.

This is Dr. Browne's ninth book. Her other titles include *Getting Unstuck, The Nine Fantasies That Will Ruin Your Life,* and the best-selling *Dating for Dummies.* Before finding her way to the airwaves, Dr. Browne was a teacher, archaeologist, and engineer in the U.S. space program. Joy keeps herself inspired by dancing, hot-air ballooning, and practicing yoga and Pilates. She is a proud resident of New York City.

Hay House Titles of Related Interest

Books

How to Ruin Your Love Life, by Ben Stein
The Love Book, by John Randolph Price
The Relationship Problem Solver, by Kelly E. Johnson, M.D.
Secrets of Attraction, by Sandra Anne Taylor
The Western Guide to Feng Shui for Romance,
by Terah Kathryn Collins

Card Decks

Heart and Soul, by Sylvia Browne
I Can Do It® Cards: Affirmations for Romance, by Louise L. Hay
Manifesting Good Luck Cards: Love and Relationships,
by Deepak Chopra
MarsVenus Cards, by John Gray
The Mastery of Love Cards, by DON Miguel Ruiz

All of the above are available at your local bookstore, or may be ordered
by visiting: Hay House USA: **www.hayhouse.com**
Hay House Australia: **www.hayhouse.com.au**
Hay House UK: **www.hayhouse.co.uk**
Hay House South Africa: **orders@psdprom.co.za**

We hope you enjoyed this Hay House book. If you'd like to receive a free catalog featuring additional Hay House books and products, or if you'd like information about the Hay Foundation, please contact:

Hay House, Inc.
P.O. Box 5100
Carlsbad, CA 92018-5100
(760) 431-7695 or **(800) 654-5126**
(760) 431-6948 (fax) or **(800) 650-5115 (fax)**
www.hayhouse.com

〜〜〜

Published and distributed in Australia by: Hay House Australia Pty. Ltd. • 18/36 Ralph St. • Alexandria NSW 2015 • *Phone:* 612-9669-4299 • *Fax:* 612-9669-4144 • www.hayhouse.com.au

Published and distributed in the United Kingdom by: Hay House UK, Ltd. • Unit 62, Canalot Studios • 222 Kensal Rd., London W10 5BN • *Phone:* 44-20-8962-1230 • *Fax:* 44-20-8962-1239 • www.hayhouse.co.uk

Published and distributed in the Republic of South Africa by: Hay House SA (Pty), Ltd., P.O. Box 990, Witkoppen 2068 • *Phone/Fax:* 27-11-706-6612 • orders@psdprom.co.za

Distributed in Canada by: Raincoast • 9050 Shaughnessy St., Vancouver, B.C. V6P 6E5 • *Phone:* (604) 323-7100 • *Fax:* (604) 323-2600

Tune in to **www.hayhouseradio.com™** for the best in inspirational talk radio featuring top Hay House authors! And, sign up via the Hay House USA Website to receive the Hay House online newsletter and stay informed about what's going on with your favorite authors. You'll receive bimonthly announcements about: Discounts and Offers, Special Events, Product Highlights, Free Excerpts, Giveaways, and more!
www.hayhouse.com